# What people are saying about
## *Taming the Office Tiger*

"After spending only a week with this miraculous book, both my life and my office have changed for the better. I finally have some time to call my own."
Og Mandino
Author, *The Greatest Salesman in the World*

"*Taming the Office Tiger* is must reading for anyone who agonizes over what to keep, where to keep it and how to find it. It provides practical strategies on organizing any office to reduce stress and become more productive."
Daniel Burrus
Author, *Technotrends*

"A valuable tool for anyone who works in an office, whether a corner suite or a corner of the kitchen. Clear, practical and in touch with today's work environment."
Thomas C. Nelson, Ph.D.
Director, Field Services Division, AARP

"As the author's father has said, half of any job is having the right tool. *Taming the Office Tiger* IS that tool! This thorough, contemporary, approachable book humanistically and flexibly supports change in an ever-changing business world. Hemphill leaves no stone unturned. It is the perfect tool …and too practical to merely collect dust on the shelf. It is a welcome and timely addition to the growing number of titles in the organization industry."
Paulette Ensign
President, National Association of
Professional Organizers

A KIPLINGER BOOK

# Taming the Office Tiger

**THE COMPLETE GUIDE TO GETTING ORGANIZED AT WORK**

BARBARA HEMPHILL

**KIPLINGER
TIMES BUSINESS**

RANDOM HOUSE

KIPLINGER
BOOKS

Published by
The Kiplinger Washington Editors, Inc.
1729 H Street, N.W.
Washington, D.C. 20006

**Library of Congress Cataloging-in-Publication Data**

Hemphill, Barbara.
  Taming the Office Tiger/by Barbara Hemphill. — 1st ed.
      p.  cm.
  Includes index.
  ISBN 0-8129-2712-5 (alk. paper)
  1. Time Management.  2. Business records—Management  3. Paperwork (Office practice)—Management    I. Title.
HD69.T54H46 1996
650.1—dc20                                         95-43156
                                                  CIP

This publication is intended to provide guidance in regard to the subject matter covered. It is sold with the understanding that the author and publisher are not herein engaged in rendering legal, accounting, tax or other professional services. If such services are required, professional assistance should be sought.

First edition. First printing. Printed in the United States of America.

*Book designed by S. Laird Jenkins Corp.*

# Dedication

With much love and appreciation to my husband (and "resident archivist") Alfred T. Taylor, Jr.

# Acknowledgements

Frequently a consulting company is named "... & Associates" to imply that the company is larger than it may actually be. In truth, that was my intent when I incorporated 15 years ago. Today the reality is that there are many "associates" without whom I would not be able to do what I do. They include my family, who has always been supportive of my efforts even when they seemed ridiculous, my friends from around the world who provide encouragement and expertise when I need it most, my business colleagues, especially those from NAPO and NSA, as well as the people who so graciously supply the services I need from designing my promotional materials to fixing my hair. And, of course, there are my clients—without whom there would be no Hemphill & Associates.

I am very grateful to Jim Grady, who provided invaluable assistance in the writing of this book, particularly the section on organizing your computer—and to Tricia Santos, who always answers my crisis calls when my computer gives me messages I don't understand!

I want to say a very special thank you to Holly Gershuny, my "assistant extraordinaire," who always goes the second mile, and is a true joy to have in our office.

A book is not a book until you have a publisher, and I am very proud to be associated with Kiplinger Books. David Harrison, Patricia Mertz Esswein, Jennifer Robinson, Dianne Olsufka, and Karmela Lejarde worked tirelessly (and sometimes tired!) to make this book become a reality.

I thank you all.

# Table of Contents

# Introduction

By Knight A. Kiplinger
Co-Editor, *The Kiplinger Washington Letter*

**S**everal years ago, we at the Kiplinger organization came across a wizard with an uncanny ability to teach people how to reduce the clutter of paper information in their personal lives, thereby increasing their productivity and peace of mind.

This wizard is Barbara Hemphill, and we are proud to be the publisher of her highly acclaimed first book, *Taming the Paper Tiger*, which has shown tens of thousands of Americans how to organize their information at home ...everything from bills and legal documents to family photos.

In her consulting practice, Ms. Hemphill also teaches business people how to get a grip on their avalanche of paper. Now her clear, easy-to-follow advice on organizing office information is available to all of us in her wonderful new book, *Taming the Office Tiger*.

I know that our company needs help in this area, and I bet yours does, too. The Kiplinger Letters, which we've written for more than seven decades, are legendary for their crisp, clear and uncluttered writing. So you might assume that our desks and offices are a similar model of spare efficiency.

Well, that's not entirely the case. Like most people, we sometimes have trouble finding just the right file, we hold onto things longer than we need to, and we sometimes feel overwhelmed by paper. The advent of computers and e-mail has helped a little, reducing the number of memos to photocopy and circulate and eliminating the little pink telephone message forms. But in the Information Age, ALL forms of communication have exploded...written, electronic and even verbal, as we talk on portable phones in places once safe from the phone's intrusion.

Barbara Hemphill can't do much about the telephone, but she has some great ideas on every other aspect of information clutter, including better organizing your computer files and voice mail system.

My grandfather, W.M. Kiplinger, believed that busy people of the 1920s were overwhelmed with too much information to read and digest, and his pioneering work in newsletter journalism was a response to this concern. As quaint as that '20s concern might seem to us today, information overload was a problem back then. It's just a vastly *bigger* problem today.

Getting better organized, at home and at the office, is a big job which, fortunately, can be divided into many small pieces and steps. *Taming the Office Tiger* will get you started and keep you on track. And it will pay you rich dividends for years to come, in improved business performance and personal satisfaction.

*Knight Kiplinger*

**P · A · R · T**

**O N E**

# Getting Centered

# First Things First: Organizing Your Thoughts

**D**o you recognize this scene? You sit down one morning determined to find your desk under that pile of papers. You pick up the first piece of paper and think of a number of reasons why you can't deal with it today. You pick up another piece, "Noooo, I don't think so…"

You remember that you haven't checked your voice mail messages. You do so, taking notes as you go. The other phone line rings. You take more notes. You switch your attention to your e-mail messages. More notes. Before you know it, the stack of papers on the left side of your desk has crept to the right side, you've got a pile of note papers sitting in front of you, and today's e-mail messages are loitering in your electronic in-box (but they're no longer flagged as "new" or "incoming").

Glancing at the clock, you realize you've got a meeting, but haven't got a clue where your notes are, or what conference room it's in. Yikes. Your morning's off to a tough start—there's just *too much* of everything!

We're all bombarded with information, much of it on paper. Even though we're now solidly in the "Computer Age," the promise of a "paperless office" has fallen flat. It's still "Paper, paper everywhere!" (So how come you can never find something to write on?)

Paper truly is everywhere in our offices. Every event in your work life, from finding a job to retiring, produces paper. Instead of freeing us from paper's clutches, modern office equipment—super-fast copiers and computer printers—has become a kind of enabler, allowing many of us to turn into our own quick-print outlet. Office junk mail—a deluge of unwanted solicitations for supplies, seminars, professional publications, and so on—is a perennial problem. But now we add to it when we tap into an on-line computer service and print out reams of information and correspondence. Sure, some is directed specifically to us, and much of it not, some is related to work, and much of it not. No matter what the situation, we might want the information "someday." But until someday comes, all that stuff sits in heaps on our desks, around our workstations, and in our files.

Certainly few people would want to do manually what we now do electronically, but we're faced with many new organizing challenges. It's tough enough to decide where to file a piece of paper, but now we've got to cope with computer files, directories, subdirectories, disks and drives. The challenge of organization is further complicated with the additions of voice mail, electronic mail, mobile phones and pagers.

What you're experiencing is the roar of the "Office Tiger." Perhaps it's only toying with you, but you know it's got you by the tail when your office is overflowing, you spend hours looking for information, and sometimes can't find it at all. Take a quick inventory. Do you:

- Have to return phone calls "later" because you can't find the information you need to have an intelligent discussion now?

- Go to meetings without information you need to make the strongest possible presentation or get the information you need from others?

- Spend time scrolling through your computer looking for an important document?

- Have files jammed with papers you haven't used in the last year or so?

- End up doing work you could have delegated if you hadn't waited until it was too late to ask for help?

- Meet in a conference room or restaurant because you're embarrassed about how your office looks?

- Forget to return phone calls?

- Blame other people for your disorganization?

- Take work home every night?

The tiger sleeps—and you have a temporary respite—when you ignore the papers, publications, messages, notes and stacks of unidentified floppies. But in the back of your mind is the fear that the tiger will awaken at any moment and rampage through your life.

You wake the tiger when you dig through piles—paper and electronic—and face disappointments, obligations, uncertainty, indecision, and the blinding reality that you are not able to do all the things you *want* to—or think you *ought* to.

So now what? You're going to confront that tiger, that's what! By following the guidelines in this book, you'll tame the tiger and regain control of your work life.

*Remember, in any organizing process, things get worse before they get better. Resist the temptation to pile everything up again and have a cup of coffee!*

## What IS "Organization?"

Let's face it—"organization" can be an extremely emotional issue! Some people resist organization because it will "cramp their style"—forcing them to become a neatnik, to sacrifice creativity or conform to someone else's standard. Others believe that time is money and that spending time to get organized is unproductive. For some, all those piles are a security blanket: "If I keep a copy of everything, I will avoid disaster." Even thinking about admitting to the need for getting organized can make people feel:

- **Fearful**—I might have to throw it out.

- **Angry**—Why should I throw it out?

- **Guilty**—Why didn't I throw it out?

*The task of organizing is boring, but unless you do it, getting what you want, when you want it, becomes very difficult.*

- **Defiant**—I won't throw it out!

- **Shameful**—I should have thrown it out!

These feelings often are symptoms of a misunderstanding about "organization."

So, what is organization? Let me begin by saying what it is not.

### Organizing is NOT a moral issue. (No matter what your mother told you!)

In fact, organizing in and of itself has no value. Its only "value" is that it helps you accomplish something important to you or your employer. The task itself is boring, but unless you do it, getting what you want, when you want it, becomes very difficult. Tom Landry, the former Dallas Cowboys football coach, once said, "My job is to make the guys do what they don't want to do, so they can be who they've always wanted to be." My role as an organizing consultant is very similar.

### Organization is not necessarily "neatness."

Remember that old adage, "A place for everything and everything in its place?" Well, that statement's only half right: A place for everything is essential, but everything in its place depends on the person and situation. Stress doesn't come from clutter—it comes from not knowing what to DO with the clutter. When I'm working, my desk is far from neat, but it takes only a few minutes to get it back in shape when there's "a place for everything!"

### Organization is not a final destination.

In the normal course of events, and particularly during crises, things will get disorganized, or simply have to change. At the simplest level, you may organize your supply cabinet. Six weeks later it looks like a disaster again. That doesn't mean it *is* one—you just didn't have time to put things away in the right place. But if you organized the supplies effectively the first time, with clearly labeled containers, it'll be simple to get things back in the right order. Also keep in mind that new responsibilities, work relationships, technologies or work spaces may force you to revise a system that used to work just fine.

### Organization does not always equal efficiency.

Efficiency refers to the mechanics of a task—the quickest way to get from here to there. But it can be a dangerous trap to spend time being efficient about things that don't matter. Organization is *effectiveness*—"Should I be doing this at all?" That means establishing priorities: What needs doing? What needs doing first, second, last?

### There is no right or wrong way to organize.

One of my biggest professional frustrations is that people are intimidated by an "organizing consultant." I often hear, "Ms. Green will meet you in the conference room," and discover Ms. Green didn't want me to see her office! Or, after meeting me, someone says, "You would *die* if you saw my desk!" Potential clients often fear that I'll pass judgement, or deem what they've done is "wrong" or "bad."

Nothing could be further from the truth. There is no "right" or "wrong" in this—there's only what works for you. What you admire about your colleague's "organization" may not work for you, and that's okay!

Here are two of my basic organizing principles:

**It doesn't matter *what* you do, but that you do it *consistently*.**

That concept can be adapted to individual styles. For example, a friend of mine constantly makes lists—but she insists on using a variety of colors and sizes of notepads.

**Does it work, and do you like it?**

If what you're handling affects other people, a third question is also appropriate: "Does it work for everyone?"

## Why Do We Resist?

So many of us feel we should get organized, once and for all. But we don't. How come? I've found four main reasons:

*There is no "right" or "wrong" in organization— there's only what works for you.*

*Are you disorganized because you don't have time, or are you short on time because you're disorganized?*

- We don't have time.
- We don't know how.
- We want to do it perfectly.
- We just don't want to.

Let's look at each one.

### I don't have the time

Lack of time is a huge factor, and something over which we don't always have control.

Not long ago, all executives, and most managers, had a personal secretary whose time was dedicated to keeping the boss organized—files kept, messages delivered, correspondence filed or sent, schedule maintained, even gifts purchased and delivered. Thanks in part to corporate downsizing, most people no longer have such help. The remaining support staff members, who each used to report to one or two people, now report to a dozen, and the managers who do survive downsizing now often do the work of two or more people.

But we're still faced with a dilemma: Are you disorganized because you don't have time, or are you short on time because you're disorganized?

People often say, "Someday I'll get organized." But often that day never comes until a crisis hits. Your best bet is to spend time organizing to avoid, or at least minimize, the crises. Organization won't prevent a crisis but you'll have a better chance of coping if and when it occurs.

You don't need to spend huge amounts of time learning new things—often we can be more successful by giving our routine a new twist. For example, if you find papers in your "In Box" that need to be filed, instead of dumping them in your "Out Box," put them in a separate "To File Box" so you don't have to sort them again. You can go one step further and identify where you want it filed, by writing the file name in the upper right hand corner. Then actual filing will be simple enough that you can delegate it to someone else, or spend of lot less of your time filing.

When I talk with potential clients, they frequently ask, "How long will this take me?" My answer? "I'm not sure, but I do know that the longer you wait to begin, the longer it will take."

### I don't know how

This is the least obvious to most people. Instead, they often criticize themselves for a lack of discipline. ("I just don't have the stick-to-it-iveness," or "I get bored!") That may indeed be part of the problem. But I've found it's usually because they don't know what to do.

When I ask convention audiences, "How many of you wish you could manage your desk more effectively?" roughly 95% of the audience raises a hand. Yet almost no hands go up when I ask "How many of you have taken a course in paper or computer file management?" Fascinating—and discouraging—isn't it, that such an essential skill is ignored by our educational systems, including the workplace?

## Dealing With the Reality of Work

### What if the "To Do" list that I created yesterday for today doesn't reflect today's realities?

In many cases, it won't. That's one of the characteristics of our fast-moving society. It means that we constantly have to reevaluate our list, revising it and verifying it against our mission statements.

### How do I handle today's crisis without completely forgetting my other priorities?

Weekly planning, weekly planning, weekly planning!

### Do I just put today's crisis at the top of the list and work my way down, as I can?

If you ask "What's the most important thing to do today?" begin doing it, then get interrupted, you handle the interruption, and then go back to your priority. That may happen a dozen or more times every day!

### What if I report to several people? What if they have conflicting priorities?

Good luck! Communication is the only answer I know. You may have to get your bosses together with you to discuss and negotiate their priorities for you. They may not even be aware that you're overwhelmed, and as long as you let them get away with it, they may find it convenient to not know, because they won't have to consider their own priorities, much less those of their associates. Point out to them that you're interested in getting the work done to the best of your ability and that working out priorities is the only way that can happen.

### If I'm going to do it, it has to be perfect

Perfectionism is one of the biggest stumbling blocks to effective organization. Often, buried within a client's cluttered office I find a vestige of organization, but it was a system too complicated to maintain. Instead of modifying a "perfect" system to make it a "possible," usable system, the client abandoned it entirely, and the result was chaos.

Procrastination is a twist on perfectionism, one *I* know all too well! It was a great revelation to me to discover that the major source of my continual temptation to procrastinate is my perfectionism. If there's something I know I need to do, but I'm afraid I won't do it perfectly, if I wait long enough to do it, fear of not getting it done *at all* will overcome my fear of not doing it perfectly. (Got that?)

### I don't want to

That's pretty straightforward, isn't it? But why *not* get organized?

A writer who had spent years in chaos finally decided she'd had enough. We spent hours sorting through boxes and piles from years past. Just as we were about to take the final step and put everything in order, she canceled her appointment. Years later she confessed to me that she realized she had always used her disorganization as an excuse for not being a productive writer. The fear of not having that excuse paralyzed her.

The negative effects of individual disorganization are multiplied at the company level and can often be assigned a dollar value. A large catering company had a very financially attractive lease on one of its kitchens. The contract stated that the company had to notify the building owner at the end of each year if it intended to renew the lease.

## *Start Organizing Early!*

● ● ● ● ● ● ● ● ● ● ● ● ● ● ● ● ● ● ● ● ● ● ● ●

Years ago after speaking at a press association meeting about how to improve organization skills, one very successful radio broadcaster came up to me and said, "You know, I've managed to accomplish a lot of things in my life, but it sure would have been easier if I had learned twenty years ago what you are teaching now." Her disorganization cost time and energy, and undoubtedly lost opportunities.

Because of staff turnover, that didn't happen, and the result was a 100% rent increase.

Granted, it's not as exciting to file the papers from completed project or contract as it was to complete the project. But the price we pay for not organizing the information can be high:

- **Missed deadlines** and resulting penalties.

- **Overlooked opportunities** and unrealized profits.

- **Time wasted** recreating a paper trail when accountability is demanded and circumstances aren't fresh in anyone's memory.

- **Lost customers** because of poor service.

- **Increased cost** from poor use of physical—and human—resources.

But the greatest cost may be to you alone. Organization will save money, time and space, and will reduce stress. As a result, productivity and quality of life will improve.

# Don't Set Yourself Up: Is it Disorganization or Unreal Expectations?

**A** potential client once called me for help. I discovered that she was required to work 60 hours a week, had just moved to a new office, lost her secretary and been given a new computer system. On top of this she was

CATHY © Cathy Guisewite. Reprinted with permission of Universal Press Syndicate. All Right Reserved.

a single parent caring for an ailing parent. Her problem wasn't lack of organization—it was a lack of *reality*. Given the demands on her time, she could never meet her expectations and her employer's.

If you make a "To Do" list day after day, and never complete it—and feel continually stressed about it, it's time for a reality check. After you make the next day's list, estimate how long you'll need to complete each task. Add on a reasonable time for interruptions, and add up the time. Is your "To Do" list realistic?

In my younger, more naive, days I believed that if I just got organized enough and managed my time better, I could accomplish everything I wanted to.

Now, I cringe when I hear someone say "You can always find time to do what you want to do." I now believe the truth is: "You can always find time to do what you want to do—if you're willing to give up something else." Life is a series of trade-offs. But nothing is forever, and it always amazes me that when I give up something temporarily, the time will come when it fits back into my life perfectly.

## The Flip Side: Getting Clear On Your Mission

Each of us has many different roles in our lives, competing for our time and attention. Sometimes all these conflicting demands can make us lose sight of our goals, and paralyze us to the point where we can do nothing. This happens in business as well, and one way that businesses keep a clear sight of goals is by having a mission statement. You can apply this strategy to your approach to work or your job—it helps you identify what's important to you and what is not. I found it enormously helpful to develop mission statements for both my personal and professional lives. I don't literally turn them into "To Do" lists. Instead, I use them as "compasses" to determine whether I'm going in the right direction: . The clearer I am about what is most important to me, the clearer I am about what is important to do from among the tasks waiting for me.

In her book, *Life is More Than Your To-Do List* (BCI Press, 301–460–3408), Maggie Bedrosian describes a discussion she had with a reader about this subject. "The idea of a mission statement is too much for me," he said. "What can you suggest that's a little more down to earth?" to which Maggie replied, "If you can't give yourself a mission statement, could you at least give yourself a

# Five Elements of Success

Even after you've identified what's important to organize, it's not always easy to do. Why? Organizing is a skill, and as in developing any other skill, it doesn't come without a price. If you wanted to be a tennis player, you could buy the best equipment, get the best coach, go to the best court, and play tennis for the weekend—but that wouldn't make you a good tennis player. You'd still have to invest plenty of time and energy in practicing and playing. The same is true for organizing. After you have identified what's important to organize, there are five essential components to implement and maintain organization:

1. Positive attitude

2. Sufficient time

3. Adequate skills

4. Proper tools

5. Ongoing practice

bumper sticker?" At its simplest, the mission statement is a clear and concise summary of what your life is for.

Here are mine. I hope you find them helpful as guides:

### For business

The purpose of Hemphill & Associates, Inc. is to:

- Encourage and assist individuals and organizations to identify and implement organizing skills in order to increase productivity, reduce stress, and reach their personal and professional goals. Methods include speaking, training, consulting, and products.
- Promote organizing in order to improve quality of life and work in our society.
- Provide the employees and associates of Hemphill & Associates with a healthy, supportive, and financially rewarding affiliation.
- Provide financial rewards to Barbara Hemphill to support a lifestyle that will allow her to continue the above indefinitely, and enable her to financially assist her extended family and other causes she deems worthy.
- Serve God in all endeavors with the hope that others will see His love through us.

### For my personal life

I choose to feel and act satisfied, thankful, peaceful, loved and loving—and to share it.

### Positive attitude

This is key—as the saying goes, "whether you think you can or think you can't, you're right."

## *Common Excuses for Not Getting Organized*

• • • • • • • • • • • • • • • • • • • • • • •

- It wouldn't stay organized anyway.
- It wouldn't make any difference.
- I have more important things to do.
- I know where everything is.
- Colleagues would think I didn't have enough to do.

Ironically, the success that comes from a positive attitude sometimes begets higher expectations that, in turn, diminish one's positive attitude. Years ago I walked into a client's office. All around the room papers were piled higher than my head. There was not an empty flat space anywhere. Files were too full to close. There was nowhere to sit. After several weeks of working together, the office looked good—and it worked.

Several years later my client called and apologized about "the mess she had made." I (somewhat fearfully) returned to her office. To my surprise and delight, I discovered a chair to sit on and plenty of evidence of organization. She had just waited too long for some routine maintenance. I reminded her of how things looked when I came in the first time. Her attitude about her organizing abilities was anything but positive, until she realized that the "problem" was now her decreased tolerance for clutter!

### Time spent now is time saved— and sometimes, money earned

Of course, organizing takes time. But in the long run, it saves time—and money. Let's say you take 12 trips per year at an average of $1000 of reimbursable expense per trip. Suppose you normally take two hours to prepare your expense accounts for reimbursement, and you procrastinate to the point that you're without the money for a month longer than necessary. If, however, you set up a system so you can fill out your expense report while you're traveling, and you put your expense-reimbursement check into an account earning 4%, you'll earn an extra $40 in interest per year—not a lot, but the cost of a good meal in many cities. More importantly, instead of spending two hours trying to recreate your expenses when you get home (and feeling guilty for several hours before you actually get around to doing it), you can spend your time on something more productive.

### Parkinson's Law states "Work expands to fill time."

Have you noticed how quickly you can get through papers on your desk just before you leave for a business trip—or better yet, for vacation? Or, if you have to get those expense reports done before you leave town, it's amazing how you can do so in less than an hour—but if you go into the office on Saturday to "catch up," before you know it, the afternoon is over and the *only* thing you got done was the expense reports.

### The rest of the game

If you're willing to accept that you can get organized, and are willing to take the time to learn, this book will help you with the skills, the tools, and the maintenance. So let's get going.

# Clutter Is Postponed Decisions

**A**ll those papers stacked up on your desk require decisions. In addition to the papers, you have to decide about computer files and e-mail or voice mail messages. But there are really only three decisions you can make about any piece of information:

- Toss it

- File it

- Act on it

Over the years, I've developed a tool I call the "Information Management Flowchart." Sounds heavy-duty, but it's quite straightforward—and helpful.

The key word here is "flow." I've found that the problem isn't that too much information flows into an office—it's that too little flows out. It gets stuck—and so do we!

This section will help you learn how to make those three key decisions quickly and well, and the accompanying "Information Management Flowchart" shows you the process, described here, that will take you through them.

## The Art of Wastebasketry

**I**t's no accident that I list "toss it" as your first option. I'm convinced that our ability to achieve goals is directly related to our willingness to use the wastebasket,

*(continued on page 16)*

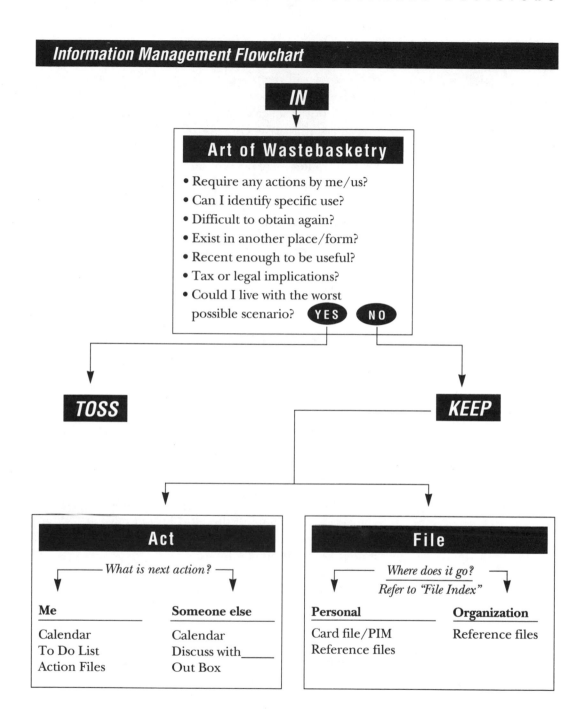

**Information Management Flowchart**

**IN**

**Art of Wastebasketry**

- Require any actions by me/us?
- Can I identify specific use?
- Difficult to obtain again?
- Exist in another place/form?
- Recent enough to be useful?
- Tax or legal implications?
- Could I live with the worst possible scenario? **YES** **NO**

**TOSS**

**KEEP**

**Act**

*What is next action?*

**Me**

Calendar
To Do List
Action Files

**Someone else**

Calendar
Discuss with_____
Out Box

**File**

*Where does it go?*
*Refer to "File Index"*

**Personal**

Card file/PIM
Reference files

**Organization**

Reference files

## Wastebasket Wisdom

*Over the years I've observed that the larger the wastebasket, the more inclined we are to use it!*

whether it's the circular file next to your desk or the trashcan icon on your computer. I've no doubt that your stress level will decrease as the amount of stuff in your wastebasket increases.

It's not practical—or perhaps even possible—to keep everything that arrives in your office. When you run out of space or can't find what you need—on your desk or in your computer—life becomes unbearable.

And, besides, Hemphill's Principle states: "If you don't know you have it, or you can't find it, it is of no value to you!"

## Fear of Throwing Out

Why is it so difficult to use the wastebasket?

### Habit

People get in the habit of "just looking" through their mail to see what is there, without throwing out all unwanted mail immediately.

### Lack of focus

If I'm not sure what information is important, it's tough to figure out what to toss.

### Fear

The "What if" game can go on endlessly: "What if someone asks me about this, and I don't have it?" "What if I don't know everything that is in this publication?" "What if next week I decide I want it?"

## Logic-Based Disposal

Determine whether you want to keep each piece of paper at all by asking yourself these "Art of Wastebasketry" questions:

### Does this require any action on my part?

Just because you receive information—even if it's from your boss—doesn't mean you need to keep it!

(She may just be cleaning off *her* desk!) If it doesn't require action, file it or toss it right away! If it's just an FYI, read it and toss.

### Does this exist elsewhere?

Is it in the library? Do you know an expert on the subject who'd be certain to have more complete information if you *really* needed it? Is the original in a file elsewhere? Do you also have a book or manual on the same subject? Is it necessary to keep a hard copy if it exists in the computer?

### Is this information recent enough to be useful?

Today, information becomes outdated very quickly. Would you want a customer to decide whether or not to choose *your* services based on a three-year-old brochure? The information in a 6-month-old magazine article about computer software has undoubtedly been superseded, as has a downloaded product review from an on-line service. In many cases, it is more appropriate to keep track of the source of the information, so you can get the latest version, rather than keeping the information itself.

### Can I identify specific circumstances when I'd use this information?

Usually, "just in case" is not good enough! Files labeled "Miscellaneous" are of little value, because there's nothing to trigger you to look there. If you can't identify how you'd use the information, it's unlikely that you'd remember you have it, let alone be able to find it later.

### Are there any tax or legal implications?

Here's where "just in case" works. Unfortunately, we're frequently required to resurrect paper that we'd much rather have forgotten. (In an IRS audit, for example!) (See Chapter 15.)

It's also wise to remember that sometimes, having outdated information in your files can create unnecessary problems. A client of mine was sued, and the company's files were subpoenaed. In one of the files was a copy of a contract which had never been executed. The prosecuting attorney was able to use that document to prove that my client's intent was wrongful, and they lost the suit. If the files had been properly cleaned, I don't believe that would have happened.

If you answer "No" to all the above questions, but are *still* not comfortable throwing something away, ask one last question:

## What is the worst possible thing that could happen if I did not have this information?

This is the key. If you're willing to live with the results, toss it. If not, keep it.

How you answer this question is significant in determining your "Retention Philosophy," discussed on page 19. Two people might answer this way: "The worst possible thing that could happen is that someone would get upset with me." One person might respond, "I'll risk it!" and throw away the item, while the other would say, "It's not

## Organizing Overview

When your desk (and your life) begins to feel out of control, remember: There are only three actions you can take on any piece of paper: toss it, file it, or act on it. The following chapters will discuss each of these steps, and more, in detail. But it's not too soon to get a sense of the whole ball game. Here are the steps you'll be following:

1. **Make sure that you can sit comfortably at your desk** and easily reach your wastebasket, "In Box", "Out Box" and a "To File Box." (See the following list of essential office supplies, the discussion on page 22 of your "In Box", and Chapter 4).

2. **Divide all the papers you decide to keep into "action" or "reference":**

*"Reference" files* contain information that you may want or need at some point in the future, whereas

*"Action" files* contain information for which "the ball is in your court."

3. **Identify an easily-accessible place (on top of your desk** or in the drawer) for action papers (see Chapters 3 and 8).

4. **Make a list of existing reference files.** File titles should be a clear indication of the contents. Put papers in their *largest* general category first, and break them down when they get too bulky (see Chapters 4 and 17).

5. **Consider a "library file" for articles you'd**

worth the risk!"—and keep it! Neither answer is "right" or "wrong," they simply reflect different tolerances for risk.

## Does anyone else need this information?

This is the last question to ask before throwing something out. Unfortunately, in many organizations, people don't know the answer—or even where to go to look for the answer. This brings me to another essential topic in effective information management.

# Retention Guidelines

I was originally motivated to write my first book, *Taming the Paper Tiger,* in an effort to answer the question, "How long do I keep ...?"

When I began organizing businesses, I discovered that "document retention" is a far bigger issue at the office than at home. Frequently, the reason file cabinets overflow and computer disks seem to multiply is that no one has made decisions about what should and should not be kept—and for how long.

like to read (see Chapter 12).

6. **Separate files that you need for historical or archival purposes** (from your regular reference files) and put them in a less-accessible space, saving your most accessible space for those files that you'll consult more frequently.

7. **Organize all non-paper items into like categories:** books, computer documentation, diskettes, supplies, etc. Use adhesive notes to make temporary labels while you are in the organizing process.

8. **Label a container or shelf for each category.** As soon as the space is filled, find a larger container or space.

9. **If you find Item A, which belongs with Item B, which you can't find,** ask yourself, "Where would I put this if I had *both* pieces?" Put whatever you *can* find there, and eventually you'll get the two pieces together.

10. **Keep asking:**

- Do I really need or want this?
- What is the worst possible thing that would happen if I didn't have it?
- What's the *next* action I need to take?
- If I wanted to find this again, what words would I think of first?
- Where can I put it so I can find it when I'm ready for it?

People often refuse to make these decisions because they're certain there's one "right" answer; as soon as they discover what it is, they'll begin to purge. Even if you consult five authorities about records retention guidelines, you may get several different answers. You're the only person who can make the final decision.

My experience is that the more organized we get, the more willing we are to *let go*. But in the case of business papers, it's important to determine what we *must* keep to protect ourselves *and* our organization.

## *Setting Up Your Own Guidelines*

First, check with your organization to see what retention guidelines already exist.

Most companies have them, but don't do a good job of letting employees know they exist. In theory the rules should be passed on from employee to employee, but in reality, that rarely happens and everyone has to figure out the rules for themselves.

It's just as bad to *have* them when they're not "user-friendly." Here's a few ways to start building retention guidelines. (If you're the boss, you'll find discussion in

## A Word About Storage Closets

Storage closets are a sore spot in many offices. I can't tell you how often I've heard a frustrated client say, "I just organized that last week, and it's a mess already!" Here are some tips to help:

- Make sure you've got the right equipment for what you're trying to store. For example, boxes of files need heavily reinforced, deep shelving, while small office supplies such as pens and staples need more, but not necessarily strong, shelves.

- Figure out the maximum quantity of each item that you want on hand and allow enough room for it.

- Put small items, such as pens, labels, staples, etc., in small containers to keep them from being scattered everywhere.

- Label all shelves and containers clearly so everyone knows where to find what they need and to put things back where they found them.

- Develop a simple system—one they'll actually use and that is easily maintained—for users to indicate when supplies are low. Consider posting a supply checklist and pen on or near the closet door.

- Assign someone to regularly maintain the storage closet.

Chapter 15 about how to effectively communicate these guidelines to your employees.)

### In the case of legal, tax or financial issues, check with your boss, general counsel or accountant.

- If you're an employee, you need to check on legal liability issues. If you don't get a satisfactory answer from your employer, then check the following resources:

- *Recordkeeping Requirements,* by Donald Skupsky ($35.00 + S&H from **Information Requirements Clearinghouse,** 5600 South Quebec Street, Suite 250-C, Englewood CO 80111, 303–721-7500).

- ARMA International, 4200 Somerset Drive, Suite 215, Prairie Village, KS 66208, 913–341-3808; FAX: 913–341–3742 offers retention guidelines for various industries.

### If you or your organization belongs to a trade or professional association, check to see what retention guidelines it can provide.

In fact, most associations don't, but they should because they could prevent each of their members from having to reinvent the wheel. At any rate, it's worth asking.

### Consider your own experience.

Often you've got to create your own retention guidelines. If you're new to a position, it'll take a year before you can make that determination, so put the old stuff in an out-of-the-way place until you can decide. Then, reflect on your actual experience with the records you *are* keeping:

- How far do you actually go back and use them?

- What would happen if you didn't have them? Are there legal consequences?

Determine a good place to put retention guidelines. A clearly labeled notebook—or a section of a procedures manual, if there is one—would work. My favorite place to put my retention guidelines is on my File Index itself. (See the discussion of file indexes, with a sample index, on page 43.)

*Handle an item only once—after you've taken it out of your "In Box."*

## Identifying What's Important By Eliminating What's Not

As I constantly remind my clients, it's not nearly as important *how* you organize, as it is *what* you organize. There is no doubt that you could effectively manage every piece of paper on your desk and every file in your computer, if that was all you had to do—but it isn't. So the real question becomes, "What can I ignore?"

## Your "In Box"

For many, the "In Box"—for paper or electronic stuff—is a holding pen for postponed decisions. You shuffle through it and don't know what to do with every item, or don't feel like figuring it out. So those items go back in the box and you shuffle them for a few more weeks, along with the new material that arrives.

The real purpose of the "In Box" is to physically separate items you haven't looked at from those you have. Let's say you sit down at your desk to look at today's mail, which you put in the center of your desk. You get part way through, and the phone rings—or someone stops by your office—and you need to find a file to get information. Another interruption follows. Before you know it, you desk is covered with papers you have looked at, and papers you haven't. Now you've got to sort through them all over again, which simply wastes time.

"In Box" to the rescue! (Fanfare, please!) Instead of

---

## Another Way to Look at It: The Tale of the Rocks

● ● ● ● ● ● ● ● ● ● ● ● ● ● ● ● ● ● ● ● ● ● ● ●

If you haven't already, I strongly recommend reading Stephen Covey's *Seven Habits of Highly Successful People*. In it, he tells the story of the professor who stands in front of his class with a jar and some rocks. He puts the rocks in the jar and then asks, "Is it full?" The class answers "Yes," but he pulls out a box with some pebbles in it, and begins putting them in the jar. He then asks, "Is it full?" Catching on to him by this time, they answer, "Probably not." And he adds some sand, and finally, takes a pitcher of water and fills the jar to the top with the water.

"What is the lesson?" he asks. They answer with comments like "You can always get a little more done," or "Use little bits of time." "No, no," he replies. "The lesson is that you have to put in the rocks first or there won't be any room." That certainly is true when it comes to managing your desk. It's very easy to be frantically busy all day long, and come to the end of the day and realize you never got to your most important task.

---

putting the papers in the middle of your desk, leave them in the "In Box"—until you're prepared to do something with each individual piece that you remove.

You've probably heard, "Handle a piece of paper only once!" Many people try that and fail, so they give up altogether. Let's adapt that old adage a little—"Handle a piece of paper only once—*after* you've taken it out of your "In Box." Use the "In Box" to hold items you haven't looked at yet. Once you've removed something from the "In Box," handle it only once to decide which of the three actions— toss, file or act—you need to take. You can then put it in a specific place, say, an immediate follow-up action pile or the "To File" box, so when it's time to take appropriate action, you'll know exactly where to look for that item.

When it comes to e-mail, take immediate action— especially deleting—whenever possible. If you're more comfortable managing paper, print out e-mail messages that require action, and handle them as you would any piece of paper (see Chapter 8).

*Barton © Cartoonists & Writers Syndicate*

## Half of Any Job Is Having the Right Tool

I grew up on a farm in Nebraska, and my father often told me, "Half of any job is having the right tool." The same principle applies in getting organized.

Let me illustrate this with an example from the home office scene—it may be one you recognize!

You come home and grab the mail. You want to have a cup of coffee while you read the mail, so instead of going to your office, you sit in the kitchen. You make piles—bills,

## A Suggestion

**For every hour of organizing, allow 10 minutes for picking up loose ends— emptying trash, putting away supplies, and so on.**

payments, catalogs, personal and professional reading, a new assignment from your manager. There's plenty of stuff for the trash—but that's on the other side of the room and you don't want to get up yet.

The phone rings—it's a colleague returning your call. You take notes at the kitchen table, after making the caller wait while you retrieve your prepared questions from the papers on the dining room table. The kids come home from school, and by now you can't remember what's what, so you scoop it all up and put it on a window sill.

You repeat this scene several times that week. You have dinner guests on Saturday, so you shove all the papers into a drawer. A few days later, you realize you can't find the notes from your earlier conversation, and you've misplaced a source's phone number. Your manager calls to discuss the new assignment and you can't find that either. You search the house for the right pile and sort through it all over again.

Sound familiar? Then it's likely that a lack of tools is the major problem. Many professionals now have offices at home, whether or not they're self-employed. One of the biggest challenges of the home office is having the right tools—a designated space and everything from a telephone to a desk, from a filing system to the necessary computer software.

Whether you're organizing an office at home or away from home, this book will help you choose—and use—the tools that will help you get organized more effectively.

## So, *NOW* What Do I Do? (Hint: Today's Mail is Tomorrow's Pile)

It's a big mistake to think that the way to "get this office organized" is to start with the backlog. Guess what happens when you start that way? While you're working on last week's stuff, today's information pours in. Unless you deal with it right away, it becomes next week's backlog. You get bogged down and give up.

Start by putting the most recent papers in your "In Box"—today's mail as well as papers that require action.

*(continued on page 26)*

## Essential Tools and Supplies for Any Office

Here's a checklist of office supplies no well-organized office should be without. We've discussed the importance of having the right tool, and certainly office supplies fall into that category. Nothing is more frustrating than clipping a magazine article for your files, and when you go to staple it, discovering you are out of staples! At that point you can make a special trip to get staples (a waste of time when you could have made one trip to pick up many supplies, avoiding lots of "special trips"). Or you have to borrow from a colleague (an interruption for both of you), or fold the corner together as a poor substitute for a staple (the pages fall apart). Wouldn't it be simpler to just make sure you have an extra box of staples?

- **Telephone.** Obvious? Perhaps, but if you're setting up a home, mobile or portable office or your own business, you have a variety of phone types and features to choose from, many of which could enhance productivity. (See Chapter 11)
- **"In Box,"** for items you haven't looked at.
- **"Out Box,"** for items to be mailed or delivered to someone else.
- **"To Deliver Box,"** if you don't have someone to do it for you.
- **"To File Box,"** for items to be filed in drawers you can't reach from your chair.
- **Container for writing utensils,** unless you'd rather keep them in your drawer. In addition to pens and pencils, they should include:
- **Highlighter**
- **Felt-tipped pen** for handwriting file labels
- **Thick marker** for marking boxes
- **Different colored pens** for calendar notations
- **Card file and extra cards,** unless you prefer an electronic "card file" on your computer or portable electronic organizer.
- **Calendar,** (paper or electronic)
- **Stapler and staple remover**

- **Labelmaker** (worth considering for files, shelves and doors)
- **Clock**
- **Ruler**
- **Magnifying glass,** if you need to read very small print.
- **Correction fluid,** even if you're "computerized," there are bound to be times when you'll need it.
- **Stationery supplies,** including:
  -business stationery and envelopes
  -mailing envelopes of various sizes
  -postcards
  -notecards
  -adhesive notes
  -address labels and return address labels
  -file folders and labels
- **Postage meter and scale.** If your office doesn't have a mailroom or you're working from home and have mail going out frequently, this will save you time at the post office. (You can buy a postage scale adequate for small mailings. For larger mailings, you may want to rent a postage meter only for $10 per month, or a meter and scale for $25 per month from Pitney Bowes.)
- **Rubber bands**
- **Paper clips and binder clips**

Put the old papers in a box under your desk, or in a bottom drawer. If you need something fairly recent, you'll know to dig through the "In Box;" it's less likely that you'll need something from the old pile—if you had, it would have risen to the top of the heap already—but you can still find what you need. As time allows, you can pull papers out of the old pile and merge them into your new system. The old papers will be easier to handle anyway once you've set up a system you understand, and in many cases, you'll probably be able to throw them away. We'll describe how to set up a filing system later on.

## *Eliminating "To Do's"*

• • • • • • • • • • • • • • • • • • • • • • • •

You can begin to eliminate "to do's" from your list by asking questions such as:

**What's the worst possible thing that could happen if I didn't do this?** Could I live with it? If so, drop that item from your list.

**Am I the only person who can do this?** If not, delegate it.

**Must it be done now?** Can I put it off for a period of time, and then reconsider its significance?

**Is there a less complicated way to do it?** For example, instead of spending hours going through old files, can I pull out the ones I know I need to begin a new system, and put the others in less accessible space in case I need them?

## What's Next?

Let's go back to the flow-chart. If you're unwilling to live with the consequences of tossing out information, you've got two options: File it or act on it.

I've discovered that if a client's desk is a major disaster in terms of the amount of paper piled on it, the filing system probably doesn't work! Clients would file much of the information they receive—*if* they knew they could find it again *when* they need it. If they're not sure, they figure it's safer to just leave the material in a heap on their desks.

But think of it this way: Often, a filing system is to an organization what a foundation is to a building. You can get away with a poorly constructed foundation for a while. You can put a fancy building on top, and lavishly decorate the interior, but sooner or later the foundation will crumble and the building will fall.

Today, information is power. If we don't have the right information at the right time, we lose opportunities. Therefore, if the filing system isn't working, our company may fall—or at least falter!

Keep in mind that the value of an effective filing system is that you can retrieve information when you need it—it's not just a place for storage! The purpose of filing anything, paper or electronic, is to create a place to put the information so that you will be able to find it again—*easily*. Bottom-line, instead of thinking "Where can I *put* this," ask yourself "Where can I *find* this?"

*The value of an effective filing system is that you can retrieve information when you need it—it's not just a place for storage!*

# Words of Wisdom Before You Begin

## Things often get worse before they get better.

This is natural and unavoidable, and it's not the time to get a cup of coffee!

## If a component of your system is weak or missing, the system will break down.

Frequently when a system breaks down, it indicates a changing focus. I guarantee that change in your job, such as a promotion, increase or reduction in support staff, relocation or travel will require restructuring or rearranging of your system.

## "Clutter is postponed decisions."

Make a decision on each piece of paper. When you're tempted to defer, ask yourself, "What am I going to know tomorrow that I don't know now?" If you *will* know more at a later date, the paper goes in your "Pending" file (see Chapter 8), for action once you have complete information. (Put a reminder on the appropriate date in your calendar to look in "Pending!")

Use the same process for e-mail or voice mail messages, and faxes.

## Continually ask, "Does it still work?" "Do I still like it?"

And, if your organization affects others, "Does it work for them?"

P A R T

TWO

# Getting Started

# The Mechanics of Filing

**D**o you hate filing? Then you'll be pleasantly surprised to discover that it can be a major stress reducer to know where to put a piece of paper, or a computer file, so you can find it when you want it. But that requires a filing *system*.

I've never met anyone who could successfully organize an office without also using a filing system—or without working with someone else who does the filing for him or her. Yet, I'm continually surprised at how few people really know how to create and maintain a system that works. Frequently, the problem is the mechanics of the system, and a little change can make a big difference.

Consider one of my clients, a social services office. I walked in and found piles of files on top of file cabinets. Apparently, the practice was to create a "new-client" file in green. When the case was closed, the file was put in a blue folder. Unfortunately, the same client often reappeared with a new problem—sometimes while the original file was still on top of the cabinet waiting for its new colored file, making it really difficult to find the necessary file.

The solution? Simple: We decided that all client files would be green. Open cases were filed alphabetically by client name in one cabinet and closed cases likewise in another cabinet—requiring only a simple move of files between cabinets with no filing system glitches to hang anyone up.

# Filing Tools: Equipment Decisions That Make a Difference

## *A Filing Cabinet*

The importance of high- quality equipment can't be emphasized enough. In fact, sometimes you're better off buying used filing cabinets, rather than new, poor quality, ones. A consultant purchased some old, but excellent quality, cabinets from a government agency for $50 each. Then, for another $50, she hired an appliance painting company to paint them bright red—to match her modern office counter tops.

When purchasing any filing equipment, make certain you get a good-quality, "full-suspension" cabinet. Full-suspension means you can open the drawers all the way so that no files are obstructed from view, and you can only open one drawer at a time so the cabinet will not tip over. These cabinets come in many styles and colors to complement your decor and available space.

You'll have a choice of a vertical or lateral file. If you're short on wall space, you may want a higher, but narrower, file. If you want additional workspace in your area, consider a two-drawer lateral file cabinet, which is shorter and wider. The top of the lateral file can hold your printer, fax machine, or working files.

Lateral files are typically arranged so that when you pull a drawer out, the files and file names are facing sideways. That may work for you if your lateral files are positioned to either side of your usual seated position, from which you will usually pull out the drawer to consult your files. But what if that's not the case and you're most likely to use the files while facing them? Most lateral drawers are designed so that you can add metal bars in the center of the drawer and arrange your files with two rows across facing you.

## Open Shelf Filing

An option most people overlook is "open shelf" filing—the kind used in doctors' offices. It can save you a considerable amount of space and money. Shelf filing goes up, not out, which can reduce floor space use by 50%.

- An open shelf unit requires only 3 square feet to hold 1,260 files (at 5 folders per linear file inch). At $15/square foot (combined space maintenance and utility costs), that's only $45 of floor space.

- Using conventional filing methods, the same number of records would have floor space costs of approximately $221.

There are people who find traditional filing systems of cabinets and files unworkable—they simply prefer cubbyholes and piles. These people may want to consider using shelves divided into compartments, or collapsible cardboard dividers, which hold the equivalent of one ream of paper and can be purchased from an office supply company. This system works for someone who likes to have large categories of information, as opposed to lots of smaller categories. For example, all the information you have about your office equipment would make one large category. If, however, you prefer to divide the information into sub-categories such as computer equipment, telephone equipment, and so on, a system of compartments would require a large amount of space and you'd probably be better off using a traditional filing system.

## Table-Top Tools For Action Files

Later on in the book, we'll cover information for which you may create special files. Appropriately, they're called "action files." For these, you may want a wire rack or portable plastic file holder which sits on the top of your desk or credenza for easy access to current topics or projects. If you have file drawers under your desk, you might want to designate one drawer to "action files." (See Chapter 8.)

## Selecting File Folders

Unless you've got a substantial amount of legal-sized paper, I recommend letter-size. They take less space, cost less money, and, because they're smaller, are physically easier to manage.

For reference files, I prefer "hanging files." These are suspended from a frame in the file drawer that allows you to slide them back and forth in the cabinet, allowing better access and preventing manila files within from sliding down in a loosely filled drawer.

If your file cabinet doesn't accommodate hanging files, you can purchase a hanging file frame that you can size to fit the file drawer.

---

## The Portable Filing Box

● ● ● ● ● ● ● ● ● ● ● ● ● ● ● ● ● ● ● ● ● ● ● ● ● ●

One of the best organizing tools on the market is the portable filing box. These boxes come in a variety of styles and prices, and can be used to create an "office" in a small space. Our company consultants always carry them in their cars when they have a client with no file space, and they need to create an immediate impact by filing the "desk papers." I use one in the "cubbyhole" beneath my desk for temporary projects which generate large amounts of paper (such as chairing a committee).

---

### Hanging or manila?

I'm often asked "How do you know when to put a manila file in the hanging file?" My guidelines are simple:

- **If the hanging file will remain in the cabinet**, and you're only going to take out the piece of paper you need, do not use a manila file.

- **If you'll be taking the entire hanging file**—such as one dedicated to a project, a committee, or a client—out of the cabinet, use a manila file inside a hanging file. Make sure to label the two files identically. This will make it easy for you or someone else to return the file to its proper place.

- **In some cases, you may want to use manila files to make subdivisions in a hanging file**. For example, the hanging folder could be labeled "Annual Meeting" and the manila folders labeled "Annual Meeting - 1997," "Annual Meeting - 1996," and so on. Make certain you put the major heading, not just the year, on the manila file so it will be refiled properly if removed from the hanging file.

If you'll be using "manila" files (which now come in many colors), and they will be used frequently, consider brands which are reinforced at the top to last longer.

### For thick files

"Box-bottom" hanging files are great for very thick files, or files with many subdivisions. These files have a cardboard strip in the bottom to accommodate thicker files. They come with strips in widths from ½" to 3".

Make sure you choose a size slightly *smaller* than the thickness of the material you are filing. If you put 2" of material in a 3" file, the material will fold over and the file will not hang properly.

### End tab file folders

If you opt for open shelf filing, or use traditional bookshelves for filing, you'll need specially designed end tab shelf file folders. These come in a multitude of styles, shapes and colors.

## Making Your Files

Labeling is the key to an effective filing system.

**Start by putting plastic tabs on the *front* of the hanging files.** Then, no matter how full the file gets, you'll still see the label. In addition, when you go to file, you can grab the plastic tab and pull, creating a blank space to put the paper. Using plastic stand-up tabs will reduce filing and retrieval time significantly.

**Stagger labels so you can read all of them without moving files when you open a drawer.** When you add a new file, it isn't necessary to change all the labels so that they are staggered in order. Just place the label so it isn't immediately in front or back of another file.

**For manila files, stick-on labels are appropriate to your needs.** If your file titles are long, use "triple-cut" (three-across) labels that are 3" long. If not, use "fifth-cut" (five-across) labels that are 2" long.

**Place file names as close to the top of the label as possible**, so they're more easily visible in the file drawer. If you are using colored, peel-off labels, put the color at the bottom of the label and the words at the top, again so you can easily read the label.

**If you're the only one using the files,** it may be simplest to handwrite your label (in capital letters) with a felt-tip pen. This will also help if you're one of those people who procrastinate about making a new file because you don't have the time or tools to make a new label.

**If the label *must* be typed** (make sure that it does and that you don't use this as an excuse for procrastinating), use an adhesive note as a temporary label. Put the sticky side on the inside of the file so it will be less likely to fall off. Then you, or someone else, can go back and make the proper label. (A labelmaker or computer program for labels is probably a better choice than typing, in terms of labor required.)

---

## *If Artwork, Posters, Etc. Are Too Large To Put In A File*

• • • • • • • • • • • • • • • • • • • • • • • •

Note in the appropriate place in the file where the materials can be located (such as "behind supply cabinet," "3rd shelf of Division Director's office," or : "flat file in Art Director's office"). If you have large amounts of such items, consider purchasing a file cabinet designed for that purpose.

---

## Using Colored Files and Labels to Advantage

Thank goodness the days of drab green and manila files are gone. Colored files and labels are wonderful for livening up your office and can provide very practical cues for visually-oriented people.

One note of caution: Unless you want to use your favorite color for all your files or your supply cabinet is consistently stocked with the same color of files, it's best to use color only when it tells a story worth telling—and then sparingly.

For example, your Administrative files might be one color, Personnel files a second color, and Project files a third color.

A doctor's office, for example, may have 20 patient

files labeled with the name "Taylor" and 20 more with the name "Smith." That office would benefit greatly from color label or file systems that quickly identify misfiles.

If you're not sure about using color, begin by using all white labels or plain manila folders. You can always add color later by adding colored folders, changing the labels or adding colored dots on the labels.

I used the latter approach in an academic publisher's office that had files for editors of various subjects. There was a separate system for each subject, such as English, Spanish and Math, within which the editors' files were arranged alphabetically by their last names.

> ## *You Can Label Anything*
> ● ● ● ● ● ● ● ● ● ● ● ● ● ● ● ● ● ● ● ● ● ● ● ●
>
> One of the great tools in the paper-management world are portable labelmakers. The laminated adhesive tape on which the labels are printed come in a variety of colors and widths. When you type out your labels on a keyboard, you can indicate the size and typestyle you prefer. The labels work not only for labeling files, but also for notebooks, shelves and file cabinets. Prices range from $50 to $500.

Things got complicated when the secretary needed to find a file for an editor whose subject she didn't know or who worked in more than one subject. We simplified the system by filing all editors' files alphabetically by last name, assigning a different colored dot to each subject and applying the appropriate dots to each editor's file label. If an editor worked in three subjects, the secretary put three dots on the file. If the secretary needed to find all the math editors, she could pull all the files with red dots.

## Filing Made Easier

The following general tips will make the mechanics of your paper filing easier.

### Avoid using paper clips.

They catch on papers when you file them, obstructing file labels and often, taking other papers with them. (You'll lose *those* papers forever!) They also take up more space than staples. It's better to staple papers together that are related, and keep a staple remover handy for separating them.

## Put most recent papers in the front of the file.

You'll see the latest information or most recent action as soon as you open the file. File cleaning will be easier, because you know the oldest papers are at the back of the file.

---

## When Phone Numbers Serve Better Than Files

• • • • • • • • • • • • • • • • • • • • • • • • •

A television producer eliminated a large file drawer of materials by making better use of her card file. For example, instead of a 2"-thick file with materials about Alzheimer's disease, she substituted one file card labeled "Alzheimer's" with the names and telephone numbers of three Alzheimer's experts, who were more likely to give her the most current information and contacts than a bunch of old newspaper and magazine clippings.

---

## Arrange file folders alphabetically.

I've found that many people resist alphabetical filing because their files are stuffed with things they never use, and they'd rather have the most important files in the front of the drawer. But if you eliminate unnecessary paper from your filing system, you'll be amazed at how quickly you'll find an alphabetically-filed file. Also, if you're out of the office, it will be easy for others to find files.

## Don't file envelopes unless the postmark date is significant.

Use your card file, calendar or planner to record return addresses. (See Chapters 5 and 6).

## Date papers you file.

You don't want to spend time consulting a company's brochure only to discover it was old and they're now out of business. Dating everything will help you or someone else know that it's time to request updated information and toss out the old.

## Stamp "File Copy: Do Not Remove" when appropriate.

For example, stamp one copy of your company newsletter, a resource directory used by the entire department, or the last copy of a form. If you'll need additional photocopies, don't waste space keeping a sheaf of copies on hand; instead, put one copy in a plastic cover to keep it clean and make copies as you need them.

### Allow at least 3" of extra space in the cabinet for easier filing and retrieval.

You know how difficult it is to find something when a file drawer is so crammed you can barely get a finger in the file. When setting up a new system, leave 20% of each drawer empty to allow for growth.

### Label the outside of each file drawer with removable tape.

Describe the drawer's contents either by subject or alphabetically, for example, "Financial Records" or "General Files, A-Mc."

### Keep a "To File Box" or pile—separate from your "Out Box"—near your desk.

Many of the papers that arrive in your "In Box" simply need to be filed. By putting them directly in the "To File Box," you'll minimize the clutter on your desk.

### Write a key word in the upper right hand corner of the paper when you put it in your "To File Box."

It's easier to make filing decisions when you've just read the letter or article, and the filing *task* will be simpler because you've already identified where to put the paper. This method is essential if someone else does your filing, because no two people would necessarily put a paper in the same file.

**Rule in my office:**

*Filing stays in the "To File Box"at my desk until it goes in the file cabinet.*

# Setting Up a System

**O**kay, you've assembled the necessary tools, and you've got a full "To File Box." All those papers have to go *somewhere*...so it's time to build your system.

## Make It Work for You

**H**ere are some tips to help you design your system. You'll find that, in principle, much of this advice will apply to how you manage your computer files, as well.

### *Keep It Simple!*

One of the biggest temptations—and most frequent mistakes—is to create too many systems. Suppose you have a job in which you wear several hats. Your first inclination may be to set up a separate system for each role, but you'll run into trouble if the information you use overlaps. If you're looking for something, you'll first have to remember which filing system it's in, and then where it is within the system. When you're filing, you may find it difficult to determine which system is appropriate for that particular piece of information.

I use a technique that greatly helps me in determining when to start a new system: If you have any question as to how many systems you should have, begin by putting all files together in one system, alphabetically. Then if you are looking for "brochure info" you will go directly to "B," instead of wondering whether you put it in the "subject" files or the "project" files.

If one category in the system becomes large enough to fill half a drawer, consider creating a separate system. For example, let's say your company decides to implement a new customer-service program. In the beginning, one file will probably be enough. But as the program is implemented and expands, more and more files will become necessary. At that point, you can pull all the files related to customer service together and put them in a separate drawer, filed alphabetically.

## File According to How You'll Use It, Not Where You Got It

A speaker at your annual convention impressed you, and you'd like to invite her to speak at a local event. Her handout might be filed under "Speaker Ideas" or "Regional Seminar Planning" rather than "Annual Convention." Or a brochure that you think is well-designed and could serve as an example of how you'd like to design your next brochure might be filed under "Brochure Ideas" rather than "Services."

## Fewer Places to Look, Fewer Places to Lose!

Most filing systems have too many files. It's easier to go

*Bart, Cartoonists & Writers Syndicate*

through one file with 20 pieces of paper than 10 files with two papers in each. It's better to put information into the largest general category first. Then if that file becomes too bulky, break it down. However, in *rare* instances, an important document may merit a separate file if there is no existing file in which it could easily be found. You could, for example, file your passport with other personal papers in a file labeled "Personal," but it's probably more helpful to have a document of that importance in a separate file, called "Passport."

## "See Also..."

I get lots of questions about cross-referencing files. If a document applies to more than one file, you can make a copy for the second, or to avoid excessive duplication, you can simply place a note on or inside the file. "See also..." written on the file folder itself will frequently be adequate.

In reality, cross-referencing takes more time than most people are willing to give. Here's where creating a filing tool called the File Index will solve the problem. With a File Index, you can quickly scan a list of all the file names in your system and pick out the places where the document could have been filed.

## Fix It or Start Over?

If you have a filing system that's not working well, or if you inherited it from someone else—whether it's in your file cabinet or in your computer—it's usually best to start over! It'll be easier to find what you want when you need it if you have one filing system that works for *you*, even if it's a small one, say, just a few files as you start!

Starting over doesn't mean days of purging old files and creating new ones. Instead, as you take documents from the old system and use them, refile them in the new system. Eventually the two systems will merge into one, or the old one will become so outdated you'll feel comfortable throwing it away. The same approach applies to creating a new computer filing system.

Keep in mind that when you take a new job, chances are you won't be given a copy of the company's information retention guidelines and it may take a year before you will be able to decide what you must keep and what you can toss. If in doubt, keep it. Just leave it in the old filing system until you're sure you won't need it.

# Your Key to Success: The File Index

The main reason paper filing systems break down is that you can file the same information under different names. Take auto information—you can file it under "Auto," "Car," "Chrysler," or "Vehicle." If several people use the same files, someone will inevitably file or refile similar material under different headings. Even if you're the only person using the file, it's easy to forget what word you used the first time.

A File Index, a list of the names of all the files in your filing system, is a crucial tool because it serves two major purposes:

**It will help you decide whether to "fix up" your existing system, or start over.** If you don't know what each file title means, it may be easier to start over. On the other hand, if you know what the title means, but you think another label would be more useful or that the file needs to be located someplace else, you can probably just rearrange your existing system.

**After you've set up a system, you can avoid making essentially duplicate files.** For example, a file for "Car" isn't necessary when you already have one for "Vehicle."

To start your File Index, make a list of your existing files. That's an easy two-person job. One person reads off the names of the files, and the other one types it in the word processor.

Look at the list:

**Does the file title tell you exactly what's inside?** If most of the file titles are mysterious, start a new system.

**Are the titles descriptive, but some overlap** such as "Car" and "Vehicle?" Perhaps there's an occasional file title that doesn't clearly describe what's in the file. In that case, revise the File Index itself, and make the physical files match the index.

By the way, if the person who decides what can and can't be purged from the files won't come *near* them, the File Index is a great way to get the decision made. You can give the decision-maker a copy and ask for input. He or she need only review the list of files with your recommendations. You can make notes by the file names such as, "I've been here for two years, and we've never used this," "Accounting keeps this in their office," or "Contains info from 1987."

## An Index You'll Use

A File Index is useful only if it's used regularly, and updated whenever you add or delete a file. Therefore, it *must* be user-friendly. These five tips will help:

### 1. Keep the File Index as simple as possible.

For example, "Airlines" (alphabetically by company) is preferable to listing each airline name. This also means that your index will not become outdated whenever you add or remove an airline.

"I've rearranged our filing system by subject."

*Schwadron, Cartoonists & Writers Syndicate*

### 2. Keep the index as short as possible.

Single space your File Index, except between each alphabetical section. You can handwrite the file titles you add to the system in the margins. If the file titles are short enough, you may want to put two columns on a page.

### 3. Maintain your index on the word processor.

Handwrite corrections on the index as you make them, and periodically update the information on your computer.

### 4. Keep copies of the index handy.

One copy should be in the front of the file cabinet itself, filed in a separate folder labeled "FILE INDEX" and

*(continued on page 46)*

## Barbara Hemphill's File Index At Work

**FILE INDEX FOR HEMPHILL & ASSOCIATES, INC.**
**ADMINISTRATION/GENERAL INFORMATION**
*Yellow Files — Lateral File Drawers #1-2*
**October 10, 1995**

Advertising Ideas
Advertising Published
Article Ideas - Business
Article Ideas - Personal
Article Markets
Articles Published about BH
  (chron order)
Articles Published by BH
  (chron order)
Artwork - Printing Info
(oversized artwork in closet)
Audio/Video Production
Brochure Development
Business Plans
Carlson Learning
CD-ROM Publishing
Certificates
Chron File
  (current month on shelf by printer)
Colleagues & Competition
Column - Syndication
Computer Notes
Consulting - H&A
  Brochure Ideas
  Legal/Business Plan Info
  Marketing Ideas
Contract Guidelines/Proposals
Copyright/Trademark
Employees
Equipment & Supplies
File Clean-Out Day
Financial Planning/Credit Info
Forms
Franchising
Get Organized News Column
  Ideas
  Master File  (one copy each issue)
I Power (see also notebook on shelf)
Library Video Network
Marketing (by City)
Marketing Ideas
Mailing Info

Mailing Lists
Meeting Sites
Mementos
Newsletter Ideas
Organizations
  (newsletters—most recent copy)
 ASAE
 Better Business Bureau
 BPIA
 Chamber of Commerce
 CSA
 NAPO - NATIONAL
 NAPO - NC
 NASE
 NSA
 NAWBO
Photographs (BH)
Procedures Manual
Product Development
Psychology of Organizing
Recycling
Resume/Bio Info (BH)
Resumes Submitted
Seminar Outlines
Seminar - BH Public
Services
Souvenir Press
Taming the Office Tiger
  Contract File
  Marketing Ideas
Taming the Paper Tiger
  Contract File
  Marketing Completed
Tax & Legal Info - General
Tax Returns 1979 - Current Year
Tax Info - Current Year + 1 Yr
    (past years in storage)
Thank Yous & Evaluations
The "To Do" Book
Warranties & Instructions

highlighted in a bright color for easy visibility, and another copy at the desk of each person who uses the file system. If your office has a large file system with many file cabinets, create a filing-system manual to keep on top of the filing cabinet for ready reference. Chances are the File Index will be too long to post on the front of the first cabinet.

### 5. Refine and update the File Index periodically.

Check all the users' copies of the index and see what files were added or deleted. Enter the changes in the word processor and print out new copies for all locations.

A filing system is only as good as the index that describes it! Remember: a File Index is a living document just as the organization it represents is living.

# Managing Names and Numbers

CHAPTER

5

**A**re adhesive notes, business cards and message slips littered across your desk and jammed into the drawers? You can't part with them, because each has a phone number, address or other miscellaneous (but important) piece of information you want to keep. Is your e-mail box similarly filled?

Perhaps you've got a dog-eared card file or computer file crammed with good intentions, or one you inherited from your predecessor. You intend to reorganize it one day, but be honest: When are you going to walk into your office and say, "Well, I have nothing important to do today. I think I'll reorganize my card file!" The solution is to just start over and create a new contact filing system.

## Managing the Information

**T**he method for starting over is the same as for starting a new filing system, whatever tool you choose. Add new names and addresses as you get them and pick up and refile entries from the old system as needed. Keep your old system nearby or on-line until you've exhausted its useful information and then throw it away or delete it, or just set it aside if you're afraid to throw it away.

The next time you get a business card, a message slip, or an e-mail message with a phone number you

47

want to keep, ask yourself, "If I want to contact this person again, what word will I think of first?" The answer is the "key word." It may be the person's last name (though in the case of family or friends, it's likely to be their first names), the name of the company, the service they provide—or even who introduced you or where you met.

People frequently hesitate to file, whichever system they're dealing with, because they can think of several key words and are not sure where to put the information. The immediate temptation is to cross-reference. But in my experience, most people don't take the time (nor is it worth it!) to enter information in several places. Therefore, by asking the question, "What word will I think of *first?*" you can usually solve the problem. The value of an electronic system, of course, is that you can search your whole database of names and addresses by key words. But that can end up being more of a time waster than if you simply identified and filed the information under a good key word in the first place.

## Choose Your Weapon

**Y**our first decision will be where to store the information. Before the days of computers, most people used a card file. Now many people use computer "contact manager" programs or portable electronic organizers exclusively. Some use one of each, for different purposes, in a combination strategy.

### *The Old Standard—A Card File*

Why choose a paper system over an electronic one? Some people just feel more comfortable with paper than a computer screen. I'm one of them. To me, one advantage of a card file is that you can enter information directly on a card as you take down a number during a telephone conversation. And I like the fact that I can look up a number without leaving the computer document that I'm using.

Another advantage of a traditional card file is that it allows you to file business cards as soon as you receive them, without having to transcribe the information elsewhere. If you choose a card file (Rolodex is the most common brand, but Bates, Eldon and Rubbermaid also make them), use a 3"x 5" size so you can staple or tape business cards right on the cards.

Even people who use a contact manager program or an electronic organizer find a traditional card file of great value. In my own case, I keep information in my card file that I want to retrieve quickly, even though it might duplicate information I keep in my computer, such as names and numbers of clients or colleagues with whom I often speak.

In my 17 years as a professional organizer, 75% of my clients have found a card file to be a valuable organizing tool—regardless of what other electronic, or non-electronic system they used.

## *Computer Databases, Including "Contact-Manager" Programs*

One of the joys of computerization is the ability to organize data so it can be retrieved in a variety of ways. A database program allows you to enter whatever kind of information you want—name, title, address, phone, fax, who introduced you, client history, and so on—and to search, sort and retrieve it by whichever criteria you choose.

*CATHY © Cathy Guisewite. Reprinted with permission of Universal Press Syndicate. All Rights Reserved.*

Contact-manager programs, such as ACT!, SHARK-WARE and TELEMAGIC, go a step further, and combine the database capabilities with a calendar and word processing capability. For example, when I'm going on a business trip to Arizona, I can use my computer's contact-manager program to retrieve every contact I have in that state, as well as print out mailing labels for them. If, while I'm in Arizona, I speak with a potential client who says, "Please give me a call next June," I can enter a reminder in my contact-manager program for June 1, and on that day, the program will present me with an automatic reminder—with or without the sound of a bell, depending on my preference. The word processor feature provides a variety of form letters that make it easy for me to write letters to my contacts in Arizona and record what I sent.

The "key word" concept also applies to a contact-manager program. Many of these systems allow you to enter information by "Primary" and "Secondary" source. For example, if a meeting planner requests information from me for a potential speaking engagement, I use the name of the association for the "primary" source, and the meeting planner's name as the "secondary." I'm more apt to recall the association name if I'm looking up the information, but if the meeting planner calls me, I can retrieve what I need by his or her name.

## Portable Electronic Organizers

Portable electronic organizers are referred to by various names, including electronic organizers, personal digital assistants, and personal information managers. In effect, they let you take your card file (and in many instances, your calendar) with you in compact form. They range from the size of a watch to a small pocketbook. The simplest model stores about 100 names, while the most advanced stores thousands of names and has word processing capability that allows you to create documents. With transfer software, you can send and receive files to and from your PC.

Some even have fax capability!

Depending on the amount of memory and the bells and whistles, these organizers range in price from under $100 to $1,000. It will cost $500-$600 to get transfer software to send and receive files from your PC.

A variety of circumstances—some explainable, some not—can cause *any* electronic device to fail. You MUST have a backup system—it's insurance you can't live without.

## My Combination Strategy

I use a combination of tools to maintain and give me access to my professional and personal contacts:

- **My contact-manager program** contains information about current, past and potential clients. I use it to keep track of services I have provided to them, as well as marketing efforts I've made with them.

- **My card file** contains names of services, such as computer repair, graphics, airlines, and so on, clients with whom I speak frequently, as well as colleagues and family members with whom I speak when I'm in the office.

- **A small leather telephone book,** which I carry in my briefcase, contains the numbers (both personal and professional) I use when I'm away from my office.

This system has developed over time and still works for me, although there are other options which would probably work as well. If I reach a point where the existing system doesn't work, I'll reconsider.

Currently, I have a desktop computer with a contact-manager program that my assistant updates while I'm on the road. If I chose, I could put the contact-manager program on my laptop so I'd have access to my database while I travelled.

When my leather phone book looks worn and needs to be redone, I could just generate a phone list from the contact-manager program. At that point, I'd have to think about what to do with family member numbers, which are not included in the program. I'd either enter them into the computer, or create a separate manual system for them.

## Other Strategies

There are probably dozens of possibilities for managing your names and numbers. Some of my clients put all their information on portable electronic organizers, others in their notebook computers, and still others rely completely on manual systems.

Remember, as with paper, the important questions are: "Does it work?" "Do I like it?"

# Making the Most of Your Calendar

Let's go back to the flowchart: Remember those three options? Toss, file, or act. Well, now you've got something you can't throw away, and you don't want to file it.

I've found that, for most people, 40% of the paper goes in the wastebasket, 40% goes in the file cabinet, and the remaining 20% requires action. How we handle that 20% has a significant impact on our productivity. The same principle applies to the information you receive in your computer.

Frequently we shuffle papers from one side of the desk to the other because when we look at the paper, it reminds us of several things we need to do. We feel overwhelmed, and we put it aside. So let's explore some ways we can eliminate that habit.

First of all, whenever you pick up a piece of paper and say "I have to do that," follow it up by asking:

**"Am I the appropriate person to take this action, or should I delegate it to someone else** (before it's too late, and I feel guilty about dumping it on someone else)?" If the answer is "No," then ask,

**"Is there a deadline on this piece of paper?"** If not, good time management may dictate that you *create* a deadline! If the answer is "Yes," you are ready to use one of the most important organizing tools in your life—your calendar.

# Smart Ways to Use Your Calendar

You can eliminate a surprising amount of paper and computer files by using your calendar. The key is to extract the information you need from the paper or the document, enter it in your calendar, and then use the wastebasket! Many people I know use their calendar as a filing cabinet, stuffing papers inside the front and back covers and in between pages. That takes lots of precious space in a briefcase, makes it harder to use your calendar and to find things, and means you risk dropping and losing stuff every time you use the calendar, to say nothing of looking less than professional.

Here are some of the ways that you can eliminate clutter by using your calendar.

## *Meeting Notices*

Let's say you receive a meeting notice in your "In Box" or your e-mail. You can enter the information—time, place, telephone number for further information—directly into your calendar. If there's more essential information on the notice than will fit in your calendar, such as an agenda and directions, you can note the name of the meeting in your calendar, and put the notice itself into your "Pending" file for future reference (see Chapter 8 for "Action" files information).

Be careful not to put so much information into your calendar that it becomes unreadable.

## *When Events Conflict*

Here's another example: Suppose you read in a newsletter about a seminar you'd like to go to, if you're in town. If you leave the notice on your desk so you won't forget, you're likely to handle that document dozens of times. But if it doesn't resurface on the appropriate day, you've accomplished nothing. Mark it on your calendar—in pencil—both on the day you need to make your reservation *and* on the day of the event. If you find there's more than one activity in a particular time slot, you can make a conscious choice about how you spend your time, instead of reacting to whichever notice happens to wend its way to the top of the pile.

## Follow-Up

If you've written a letter, and you need a reply in two weeks, make a note in your calendar, "Heard from John?" This way, you use your calendar not only as an appointment calendar, but as an effective follow-up tool. If there are specific materials you want to check when you follow-up, make a note in your calendar of where they are, for example, "See XYZ file."

## Appointments With Ourselves

Many of us are great about using our calendar to make appointments with others, but rarely make appointments with ourselves. Yet I've found that the people who are most successful in managing their time and reaching their goals are those who make appointments with themselves to complete specific tasks and check on specific issues.

Let's say you attend a meeting, and agree to complete a certain task. Instead of writing a note on the legal pad you've got with you and hoping it will resurface when you need to remember, make a quick calculation about when you need to begin work on that task and mark it on your calendar. You avoid creating additional pieces of paper, and you'll be reminded at exactly the right time (see Chapter 8 for information on "reminder notes" and "action" files).

If there's something specific you want to do for yourself—like clean out your file drawer or spend time on your "To Read" pile, (see page 74)—make an appointment with yourself, just as you would with someone else. Some people hesitate to use this approach because they're afraid of becoming compulsive. They shudder at the thought of talking to a colleague and saying, "I need to go now. I have to catch up on my reading!" I am NOT suggesting such inflexibility! Using your calendar as a time

*The people who are most successful in managing their time and reaching their goals are those who make appointments with themselves to complete specific tasks and check on specific issues.*

*Keep in mind that you don't have to use every tool that a particular product includes. Choose the ones that work for you, and omit the others.*

management tool helps you be realistic about your time. If you've blocked out an hour to write the report from your last committee meeting and decide something else is a higher priority, you *can* choose another time to write the report.

## Choosing Your Calendar or Planner

I've never met anyone comfortable with the way they managed their paper and their time who didn't also have a calendar or planner they counted on. Choosing from the dozens of calendars and planners on the market can be overwhelming, let alone learning to use one. But doing so is a major step toward gaining control of your work and personal life and should be very high on your priority list.

When evaluating your calendar, ask those (now-familiar) questions: "Does it work?" "Do I like it?" If either answer is "No," begin now to find a replacement. You'll probably use it 300 days out of the year, and it *can* be a big investment.

Some companies require, or at least strongly encourage, employees to use a particular product. Over the years I've seen many dusty planning books laying on shelves because they simply didn't work for those individuals. A better approach is to look at the people around you that you admire and gather ideas from them. But be realistic: Don't assume that because a product is perfect for them it will be for you. Ask them what they like and don't like about their system, and determine which of those things matter to you.

I've never met anyone who thought their calendar was perfect—it's too big to fit easily on a desk or in a purse, briefcase or shirt pocket, or it's too little and doesn't have enough writing space, or even that it doesn't come in the right color! As with many other things in life, there are trade-offs.

Choose the calendar or planner that meets the greatest number of your needs, and adapt it. The discussion that follows will help you make the big decisions about choosing a calendar or planner.

## *Adapting Your Calendar*

Shortly after Christmas a few years ago, I was sitting on an airplane next to a woman who was browsing through a beautiful red leather planner. She sighed audibly, and I asked her what was wrong. "Oh," she replied, "I must be hopeless. My husband gave me this beautiful calendar for Christmas to help me get organized, and I don't even know how to use it!" We spent the next two hours discussing how she could adapt it to meet her needs, and when we parted at the baggage claim she asked, "Did my husband arrange for you, too?"

If you're lugging around a big calendar, for example, but you like lots of writing space, use adhesive notes to write reminders and stick them to the appropriate calendar pages. When you've completed the task, throw the note away. Remember that adhesive notes come in many sizes. I use the 4" x 6" size for taking notes from a telephone call when I'm on the road and a 3" x 5" for the list of office supplies I need. That way, when I'm running errands and pass a supply store, I can pick up the items on my list and avoid making a special trip. (Another option, of course, is to order all supplies by phone or fax and have them delivered.)

Perhaps you have found a terrific weekly calendar, but you also need to look at the entire month. (Add a peel-off pocket to the front or back of the weekly calendar, and put a small monthly calendar in the pocket.)

Many companies have begun calling their calendar products "planners" because they contain more tools and

*CATHY © Cathy Guisewite. Reprinted with permission of Universal Press Syndicate. All Rights Reserved.*

information than just a calendar. These include project planners, telephone call logs, forms for recording meeting minutes, or even geographical or overseas travel information. But keep in mind that you don't have to use every tool that a particular product includes. Choose the ones that work for you, and omit the others.

You can spend $15 or more than $200 on elaborate planning components, but an expensive one won't necessarily work better than a lower-priced one. There are even planners that double as purses and briefcases! If you want more than a calendar, but can't find a planner that meets your needs, design your own. It's as simple as taking a three-ring binder and adding subject dividers. You can create your own forms, or use predesigned ones from various companies to suit your needs. Cost doesn't necessarily correlate with quality or effectiveness.

## Daily, Weekly, Monthly (or More?)

The first decision you need to make when picking a calendar is how much of your schedule you want to see at one time—a year, a month, a week, or a day or a combination. (I prefer a combination, which I describe below.) Time-management experts say that scheduling time in weekly blocks is the most effective way to be *proactive* with your life rather than *reactive*. My personal experience supports that.

For years I used a daily calendar that had the advantage of providing lots of writing space. I selected one in which I could schedule the day's fixed appointments on the left-hand side of the page and write my "To Do" list on the right-hand side, including phone calls to make, follow-up actions, and so on. The front of the calendar provided a monthly calendar where I noted "non-negotiable" appointments around which I manipulated the rest of my schedule—business travel, major events, important family commitments, etc.

However, in recent years I've found that I must make more *choices* about what I will and will not do. A calendar with a weekly format works better for me now because I can track how I am meeting my priorities. Say, for example, my goal is to exercise three times a week—something many of us want to accomplish during the work day, but have difficulty getting around to. I make an appointment with myself—and check it off when I get it done. If I get to mid-week and there are no checks by exercise, I know I have to get moving!

## *Paper or Electronic?*

Another decision you need to make is whether to use a paper calendar, a portable electronic organizer with calendar features, or a computer program for your desktop or laptop computer.

I know people who've never successfully used a paper calendar who find a computer-based program indispensable. Like paper calendars, these come packaged in a myriad of ways, from part of a word-processing package to a separate, add-on program or a hand-held device.

One big advantage is the ability to search for information in a variety of ways. For example, if you want to find every contact you've had with a particular client, you can search by the client name and get all the information you need within seconds. These programs allow you to print out hard copies of your calendar, and it's easy to make backup copies for protection. If your computer is networked with the person who schedules your appointments, it's simple to share information without transcribing data from one calendar to another. Some programs have time management features, including "To Do" list and tickler functions. One client selected a computer-based calendar because he had difficulty reading his own handwriting!

On the other hand, many people who used paper versions successfully, but felt compelled to try the latest technology, missed the paper. I fall into that category. I feel a sense of security in being able to hold my schedule, and knowing I can always access it, without depending on technology. I use different colored pens to indicate different things: Red, for example, indicates when my youngest child will be home from school; purple, my husband's trav-

*(continued on page 62)*

## A Look at My Calendar

Here's a sample of my calendar. I use the yearly section for an overview of what lies ahead (last six months shown below). Abbreviations and short descriptions let me know where I'll be (Boston on the 7th, for example), family schedules (I use a different color pencil for each family member), and important events (Pat H. birthday on 4th). Appointments, daily "to do's" and projects go in the weekly section (left-hand page shown opposite) under my different roles. Expense notations are on the right-hand page not shown here.

| | SUNDAY | MONDAY | TUESDAY | WEDNESDAY | THURSDAY | FRIDAY | SATURDAY |
|---|---|---|---|---|---|---|---|
| | | | | | | 1 _CANADA DAY_ | 2 |
| JUL | 3 | 4 PAT H. _INDEPENDENCE DAY_ | 5 | 6 | 7 ADIE/CHUCK BOSTON | 8 | 9 |
| | 10 | 11 | 12 RON~MARIE | 13 | 14 BETTY | 15 | 16 |
| | 17 | 18 | 19 ABERNATHY | 20 | 21 | 22 PAM | 23 |
| | 24 | 25 BOOK FAIR | 26 | 27 | 28 | 29 | 30 BOBBIE |
| AUG | 31 | 1 | 2 WINSTON-SALEM | 3 | 4 —ASHEVILLE | 5 —— | 6 NAPO BOARD |
| | 7 | 8 | 9 —VACATION | 10 —— | 11 | 12 | 13 |
| | 14 JOUA-21 | 15 | 16 —VACATION | 17 —— | 18 | 19 | 20 |
| | 21 | 22 —ATLANTA | 23 —— | 24 | 25 | 26 | 27 DUKE |
| | 28 | 29 HAIRCUT | 30 | 31 | 1 | 2 | 3 |
| SEP | 4 | 5 _LABOR DAY_ | 6 _ROSH HASHANAH_ | 7 HEIDI TO SCHOOL | 8 | 9 CSA | 10 AT/DRILL |
| | 11 AT/DRILL | 12 DUKE | 13 AT/BH ANNIVERSARY | 14 | 15 _YOM KIPPUR_ | 16 | 17 |
| | 18 | 19 | 20 | 21 NATION'S BANK NCSU | 22 ASJA —ASHEVILLE | 23 —— | 24 |
| | 25 | 26 | 27 HOWARD COUNTY | 28 | 29 WASH DC | 30 —— | 1 |
| OCT | 2 —— | 3 RADIO TOUR — | 4 GET ORGANIZED | 5 | 6 WEEK — | 7 | 8 |
| | 9 | 10 CHARLOTTE COLUMBUS DAY OBV THANKSGIVING DAY (CAN) | 11 | 12 _COLUMBUS DAY_ | 13 BEN~21 HEIDI | 14 | 15 STANTON |
| | 16 —— | 17 | 18 NAPO | 19 | 20 NCSU | 21 | 22 |
| | 23 | 24 | 25 | 26 | 27 | 28 | 29 |
| NOV | 30 —— | 31 HALLOWEEN | 1 ELECTION DAY | 2 | 3 | 4 —NAPO RETREAT | 5 —— |
| | 6 —— | 7 | 8 | 9 ASTD | 10 | 11 VETERAN'S DAY | 12 |
| | 13 | 14 | 15 WASH DC | 16 | 17 | 18 | 19 |
| | 20 | 21 NAPO-DC | 22 | 23 HEIDI | 24 THANKSGIVING DAY | 25 | 26 |
| DEC | 27 | 28 CHANUKAH BEGINS | 29 | 30 | 1 | 2 | 3 |
| | 4 | 5 —FT. LAUDERDALE | 6 —— | 7 —— | 8 | 9 | 10 |
| | 11 | 13 | 13 | 14 | 15 | 16 | 17 |
| | 18 | 19 | 20 | 21 HEIDI —— | 22 | 23 | 24 |
| | 25 | 26 | 27 | 28 | 29 | 30 | 31 |
| | CHRISTMAS DAY | | | | | | |

YEARLY PLANNER

**PLANNING FOR THE WEEK OF:** AUGUST 22

## WEEKLY LISTS OF ACTIVITIES BY CATEGORIES

| H & A | SPEAKER/WRITER | NAPO | FAMILY |
|---|---|---|---|
| TRIANGLE AD | HEARD FROM TINE? (CW) | CALL CHRIS (C) | CHAIRS / BED TO |
| NCSU | NCSU SEMINAR PLAN | LETTER TO ARIZ | CHURCH 878-9385 |
| BROCHURE COPY | TAMING CORRECTIONS | BY-LAW REVISION | HEARD FROM MARGARET? |
| VIDEO FEEDBACK? | | CONTRACT | MORTGAGE APPLICATION |
| FLYERS RE DUKE | | NEW ADDRESS | CALL LANDSCAPER |
| | | | |
| | | | RSVP - SK WEDDING (H) |

## DAILY THINGS-TO-DO

| MONDAY 22 | TUESDAY 23 | WEDNESDAY 24 | THURSDAY 25 |
|---|---|---|---|
| TAMING CORRECTIONS | MARY HIGGINS | CALL RENETTE | CALL CHICAGO (H) |
| BOB BAILEY | 924-5267 | 834-3722 (W) | |
| 700-902-8202 | ALEX - GOING TONIGHT? | CHRISTY - NAPO? (CW) | |
| MOLLY GLANDER | JAN SWANSON | 600-322-9753 | |
| CALL RON FALKIN | 800-790-1342 | | |
| REMAX 242-3100 | INFO TO STAPLES | | |
| CALL GREER — | | | |
| SEE 8/11 | | | |
| CALL SUSANNE | | | |

## APPOINTMENTS

| | | | |
|---|---|---|---|
| DADDY'S BIRTHDAY | | | |
| 7: | 7: | 7: | 7: BREAKFAST / CLUB K.C. |
| 8: | 8: | 8: | 8: |
| 9: | 9: NATION'S BANK | 9: | 9: NCSU - DELIVER ART |
| 10: | 10: ROD - 829-6633 | 10: | 10: |
| 11: | 11: | 11: | 11: |
| 12: | 12: | 12: | 12: MOLLY / KAY |
| 1: | 1: | 1: | 1: RE COVEY |
| 2: HAIRCUT | 2: | 2: | 2: |
| 3: | 3:30 NCSU - PAM SMITH | 3: | 3: |
| 4: | 4: 2190 BERLIN Rd. | 4: | 4: |
| 5: | 5: 501-3470 | 5: | 5: |
| 6: | 6: | 6: | 6: |
| 7: | 7: | 7: | 7: |
| 8: | 8: ENNIS | 8: | 8: |
| 9: | 9: | 9: | 9: |

(Monday column: WRITING written diagonally)
(Wednesday column: SUCCESS SEMINAR GREENSBORO HILTON written diagonally)

PLANNER PAD®

H=Hold     LM=Left message     CW=Calls waiting     D=Discuss     C=Call el schedule, and green, my writing deadlines. I always have a bottle of liquid paper in my desk for when plans change—and I write tentative plans in pencil.

## Should You Have More Than One Calendar?

If your business life is basically "nine to five," then you'll need a calendar at the office. You will also need a calendar for your personal life, and you might need to take it with you to the office, since most people end up doing personal business sometime during the work day. But chances are your business and personal life overlap, as is true for me, and you don't want to run the risk of not having one of your calendars with you when you need it. If that's the case, then your best option is a master calendar that reflects both areas of your life and that you carry with you virtually all the time. For example, my haircutter is in high demand, and I need to schedule her weeks in advance. I take my master calendar with me to each appointment so I can schedule my next one while I'm there, thus avoiding an extra telephone call.

In addition to your master calendar (and other "satellite" calendars), you may have other calendars for specific functions. For example, a calendar on my office wall indicates my travel schedule so colleagues know when I'll be available. Many offices use a huge wall calendar to schedule projects with intermediate deadlines. One caution: If you put it up, use it consistently, or you risk people not taking deadlines seriously.

## Combining Your Phone Book With Your Calendar

Everyone I know carries at least *some* phone numbers and addresses at all times. In a looseleaf planner, you can carry the same telephone section forward from year to year, while in bound ones, you have to recopy that section each year. Manufacturers of the latter style contend that it's a good practice to annually purge numbers you carry with you. That's probably good advice, but many people would never do it. I've frequently had clients who carry two years' calendars because they didn't have time to recopy the phone numbers and addresses. Although the planner I use has a section for phone numbers, I carry and use a separate phone book—a small leather book that fits in any purse I carry. It even works for social occasions, when I won't carry my planner but may still be networking and want to make notations of people I meet.

## How My Calendar Reflects My Roles in Life

Choosing your calendar is a personal decision. The main thing is to choose it and use it—consistently!

I personally use the Executive Planner Pad which is 8½" x 11" and is about a half inch thick (see the sample on pages 60-61). It allows me to combine my calendar and my "To Do" lists (discussed in the next section) into one book that's small enough to easily carry in my briefcase.

It provides two pages for each week. The pages are divided into thirds horizontally. The bottom third is for noting fixed appointments. The middle third is for noting the things I want to accomplish during the day, such as phone calls to make, letters to write, and so on. I can use the top third to list current major projects with notes about what I need to accomplish that week.

In order to work on the issue of balance in my life, I have found it helpful to use the top third to identify the major roles in my life and what I expect to accomplish that week, based on the principles of Stephen Covey's *First Things First*. For example, my current major roles include business owner, communicator (writing, speaking), National Association of Professional Organizers member; National Association of Women Business Owners Chair, wife/household manager, family member, and friend/neighbor. At the end of each week, I look at all my roles, and determine what I hope to accomplish in each of these roles during the week. Some roles may have no

*Choosing your calendar is a personal decision. The main thing is to choose it and use it— consistently!*

goals in a specific week. For example, "friend and neighbor" may be blank if I am going out of town on business. See the discussion below for more on coordinating your calendar with your "To Do" list and your "action" files.

## *Safekeeping for Your Calendar*

Whatever calendar you choose I encourage you to do whatever you can to minimize losing it. If it's electronic, on your computer or in an electronic organizer, back it up, as you would any other computer file. If it's paper, put a note in the front saying "Return for Reward" with contact information that you feel is safe to provide, probably your work address and/or phone number.

# Your "To Do" List

## How Your "To Do" Lists Can Eliminate Clutter

**D**esks are often cluttered with pieces of paper we keep as a reminder of something we want to do—review the insurance coverage, update the marketing plan, or revise the company policy manual. To eliminate clutter, make a "To Do" list of projects you want to complete, and file the information away until you are actually ready to take action.

For example, say I get a catalog in the mail that has information about a product I am thinking about buying. Instead of cluttering up my desk with the catalog, I can make an entry on my "To Do" list that says "Purchase new widget." I can then file the catalog with my other catalogs (with a page number of the widget on the front) or file it under "Shopping Information" or "Widget." If you are afraid you will forget where you filed the catalog, make a note on your "To Do" lists that says "See catalog in _____."

## *To Do or Not To Do— (THAT is the Question!)*

Perhaps the toughest part of organizing is deciding what to do and what not to do. In *First Things First,* Stephen Covey, with Roger and Rebecca Merrill, suggests that how we spend time can be divided into four quadrants:

- (I) Urgent and Important.

- (II) Important but not Urgent.

- (III) Urgent but not Important.

- (IV) Not Urgent and not Important.

"Urgent" is usually determined by an outside influence such as a deadline imposed by your boss. "Important," on the other hand, is determined by our values—what really matters to us, what we want to accomplish at work and home, such as completing a project on time and with high quality, hiring a new assistant, getting a new job, spending more time with your family, and taking better care of your body.

For example,

**Quadrant I** could be "It's April 13 and I haven't done anything about my taxes."

**Quadrant II** could be exercise. (If you don't exercise, but your doctor tells you to lose 20 pounds or risk a heart attack, it becomes a Quadrant I!)

**Quadrant III** could be a telephone call from a sales rep while you were working on your monthly analysis report.

**Finally, Quadrant IV** would be that lunch you didn't *really* want to have with the person you didn't have the guts to say "no" to!

I attended one of Stephen Covey's seminars, and he asked us to "name one thing that, if you did it consistently, would improve the quality of your life." Try it yourself. If you're like most people, the answer—whatever it is—falls into Quadrant II, "Important but not Urgent."

*CATHY © Cathy Guisewite. Reprinted with permission of Universal Press Syndicate. All Rights Reserved.*

I learned that I had eliminated most of Quadrants III and IV from my "To Do" list—except when I was procrastinating, for example, cleaning off my desk when I planned to look for some new sources for clients. But to my horror, I discovered I virtually *lived* in Quadrant I. Everything I was doing was not only important to me, but urgent, too, because I was trying to do too much and I was always on deadline.

What's the answer? I'm still learning, but here are some things I am sure of.

- Deciding whether "to do or not to do" requires continually checking your "To Do" list with your mission statement (see Chapter 1).

- The more I do the less I enjoy.

- Just because I choose not to do something now doesn't mean I can't do it later.

- Sometimes I can get satisfaction by doing something less than perfect.

## 2 Types of "To Do's"

• • • • • • • • • • • • • • • • • • • • • • • • •

"To Do's" come in two major categories—those that must be done at a specific time (such as make airline reservations for an upcoming trip) and those for which you have not yet established a formal deadline. The former should be noted in your calendar on the appropriate day, and the latter in a designated place to be reviewed periodically for incorporation into your calendar.

For example, some of my daily "To Do" list is created in my calendar, on the day when I have decided that I will do it. For example, I may attend a meeting at which I agree to submit a report by a certain day. I enter the "Write XYZ report" on my "To Do" list in my calendar on the day I will write it. If I'm not sure when I will write the report, I put it on my master "To Do" list, which I review weekly to make my daily "To Do" lists for the week. Of course, these often have to be revised as the week progresses.

I can choose to do a Quadrant II activity today, (such as spending time with my daughter who will be leaving in two days), knowing that I'll be in Quadrant I with work tomorrow—but it is my choice!

## Where to Keep it

Your "To Do" list can be located in various places—a section of your calendar, such as I mentioned in describing my Daily Planner, a computer file, a separate notebook or pad, or even a wall chart or whiteboard (with erasable markers). As with other systems I've described, **consistency** is crucial, so develop a system that'll be easy to use. If your system is not portable, make sure you have a method of incorporating the ideas that occur to you when you are not in your office such as carrying notecards in your pocket or briefcase. Then incorporate them into your system when you return to your office.

## *Organizing Your "To Do" List*

One basic principle when organizing anything is to "put like items together." This technique works for your "To Do" lists as well. I've found it helpful to categorize my "to do's" by roles as I described previously in the section on calendars. Two other favorite categories of mine are "errands" and "books." I can minimize trips around the city to accomplish errands, and I have a list of books that I want to see whenever I go to the library or bookstore.

## *Looking at Your Accomplishments*

A friend of mine says he makes lists of things he's already done because it's fun to check them off! If you constantly make "To Do" lists that you don't complete, try the exercise of making a list of what you *did* accomplish. What quadrants were they in? Identify those things you could have:

- **Eliminated from your list**—did you do them to avoid doing something else?

- **Delegated**—were you the most appropriate person to do them?

- **Simplified**—written a quick e-mail message instead of a formal letter.

# Action Into Files—or Piles?

**A**lthough you can eliminate mounds of paper from your desk by using your calendar, "To Do" list, card file or computer database program, and your "reference" files, you'll still be faced with papers that require action.

If you don't have much left on your desk after tossing and filing, you may be quite comfortable with just one "To Do" pile—or maybe three piles, prioritized by urgency. However, in my own case and those of many people with whom I work, a few piles simply are not enough given the many hats we wear and the workloads we bear.

You can sort the remaining paper in a variety of ways. One would be to sort them by project or activity, such as "trip" or "meeting." But there are many individual and miscellaneous papers, unrelated to a larger project, that require action such as making a phone call to inquire about a new product or writing a letter to thank a colleague for referring a new client. These can be sorted into files—or piles, if you prefer. But how?

Remember that clutter is postponed decisions. To decide which file, ask yourself, "What is the *next* action I need to take on this piece of paper?" The word *next* is crucial: There may be a dozen things that paper reminds you to do, but you can only do one at a time.

Typical answers to that question are "call," "write," or "read." You can create an "action" file—or pile—for each category. Your answer will tell you which "action" file or pile you need to create and use.

## How It Works in the Real World

Occasionally it takes time to figure out your next action. For example, you received a memo from Terry with questions about a contract. Your initial reaction may be, "I have to call Terry," but you realize you need to review the contract first. It's in the filing system, but you don't know where. Your assistant—who does—is away from his desk! Terry's memo requires three actions: get the contract; read the contract; call Terry.

**The first action would be to put the memo in your "Out Box"** with a note to your assistant to get the contract by a certain time.

**When the contract arrives in your "In Box,"** you take it out and place it in your "Read-Urgent" file—or if reading it will only take a few minutes, put it into your "Call" file and you can read it just before you make the call. In either case…

Harris, Cartoonists & Writers Syndicate

**You can make a date with yourself in your calendar** with a notation as to where you put the memo—"R" for read or "C" for call.

## Out of Sight, Out of Mind?

"All well and good," you say, "but if I put a piece of paper in a file, I'd never see it or do it." Well, okay, if you have fewer than 20 pieces of paper on your desk, the "action" file system I'm proposing isn't necessary. But as the volume of paper on your desk increases, your ability to find the paper when you need it decreases, and you're more likely to find it if you put it in an "action" file.

One advantage of gathering like actions together is that you could increase your productivity. If, for instance, you're making one phone call, you can probably make another in a few more minutes if you don't have to spend time looking for the paper you need to make the call.

## Suggested Categories

Here are descriptions of a number of categories for action. Don't be intimidated by the number of categories; you won't need them all, and you might need others that aren't described.

If, as you read through the list, the whole idea seems overwhelming, choose a few categories that particularly appeal to you and try them. "Call," "write" or "read" might be just enough to start with. "Calls waiting," described below, has been a favorite of my clients through the years; the problem of finding a piece of paper you need to discuss with a caller seems to be a common one.

### Call

Many times the next action required on a piece of paper is a telephone call. In addition to putting the paper in your "Call" file, you may want to make a note on your calendar on the day you need to make the call. Using a symbol such as "C" will remind you that there is additional information in the "Call" file.

### Calls waiting

How many times have you made a telephone call to someone and they weren't in, so you leave a message on their answering machine or voice mail and put the piece of paper on your desk? Then days or even weeks later, you get a call that begins, "This is Jerry returning your call." You get a knot in your stomach as you frantically try to remember why you called him—or even who he is.

If you have the paper in your "Calls Waiting" file, you won't risk embarrassment or have to make another call because you couldn't find what you needed.

If you need to hear from that person by a specific

date or time, put a note in your calendar or your day's "To Do" list, "Heard from Jerry?" with a "CW" to remind you where you put the paper in question.

If you were simply returning a call and the ball is now in the other person's court, just leave it in the "Calls Waiting" file for a while. On the paper, note the date you returned the call, so you will know how long it has been. If you get no response within an appropriate length of time, toss it.

## Computer entry

Some of the papers in your "In Box" or floating on your desk contain information that needs to be entered into your computer. It's more time-effective to make several entries at the same time—or delegate the task to someone else. When you've entered the material from this file into the computer, either throw out the papers, pass them on to the next person who needs them, or if you must save them, file them in the appropriate "reference" file.

Why, you may ask, if I'm helping you tame your office tiger, would I suggest you keep paper after you've entered the information in your computer? There are instances when you need to keep the paper. For example, you might enter your expenses into the computer, but you need to keep the paper for tax purposes. But always ask, "What's the worst possible thing that would happen if didn't have this piece of paper?" If you can live with it, toss it!

## Discuss

Often we can't act on a matter until we've discussed it with someone else. We all have certain people with whom we routinely discuss issues. The "Discuss" category will contain several subcategories including those persons' names filed alphabetically by first name or title, such as "accountant." Here's where I like to use colored files, assigning one color to each of the people I talk to regularly, so I can recognize the appropriate file quickly when someone steps into my office or I get a phone call.

### Errands

Many of our "To Do's" need to be done outside the office, such as getting a document notarized, checking out a new office supply store, getting a color copy, or checking out a resource at the library. If you traditionally have dozens of errands, you could organize them into subcategories by geographic location, deadlines for completion or by type of errand.

### Order

If you frequently use mail order catalogs or if you're responsible for ordering office supplies or equipment, this might be a useful category.

### Pay

This file is for bills to pay. If appropriate, you might use it for expenses for which you are entitled to reimbursement by your company. Because I have a home office, I pay both my personal and business bills there, and I divide my bills accordingly into three categories: Business, Personal, (which I pay monthly) and Donations (which I consider separately once each quarter).

### Pending

This category can be called many things, such as suspension, bring-up, or tickler file. It's for papers you'll need at a specific date in the future. For example, if you sign up for a seminar and receive your tickets with a map and instructions about how to get to the seminar, put the information in your "Pending" file and note a "P" in your calendar on the day you will need it.

Remember, that's "P" for "Pending," not for Procrastinating! When you're tempted to put something here because you're not sure *what* to do, ask yourself, "What am I going to know tomorrow that I don't know today?" If the answer is "Nothing," you need to look further into the issue to find out what other category the paper truly belongs in.

You can create pending files in three ways:

- **A system of 31 files (one for each day of the month, as well as files for upcoming months).** If you use this system, it's not necessary to note in your calendar the date when you'll need something, but you *do* need to check each day's "Pending" file. When I tried this approach, I found I wasn't consistent about that—especially when I was traveling, since I wasn't in my office to check the file.

- **One file for each month and one for "Next Year."** This is the system I use—I check the file at the beginning of each month or at the end of the previous month. All the items in the pending file that have to be retrieved on a particular day are noted in my calendar with "P."

- **One file in which you arrange items chronologically.** This is appropriate only if you don't have many pending issues. Be sure to put a note in your calendar to remind you to retrieve the paper you need.

### Photocopy

Often, you can't take the next action on something until you make a copy of the paper. If the machine isn't readily available, it's helpful to have a file to hold the pa-

---

## Managing Your "To Read" Pile

Overwhelmed by the piles of reports, magazines, journals and newsletters sitting around your office? Consider these tips:

- **Accept the fact that you will probably never be able to read everything** you would like to (or think you ought to)!
- **Read with a pen in your hand.** On the front cover of the publication, note the page number and subject of articles that particularly interest you, so you can find them quickly.
- **Check the table of contents in a magazine** when it first comes in. Tear out and staple together the articles you want to read. Put them in a file folder in your briefcase to read when you are waiting for an appointment or riding the subway.
- **Avoid the "perfectionist syndrome."** Instead

of putting aside that newsletter until you can read it perfectly, and then discovering you're reading the information too late to be of value, scan it for time-related information when it arrives.

- **Delegate your reading.** If you have support staff, train them to scan magazines and journals for articles that might be of interest to you—and highlight particular thoughts.
- **Create a separate filing system for articles you want to read**—your personal "Library." Your motivation to read the articles and your ability to determine their value will be much greater if they relate to a current problem. You'll find them much more quickly there than in a pile of magazines behind your desk!

pers that need copying, which you can take with you when you go down the hall, to the next floor or when you make a trip to the library or other "copier place."

If you work from a home office and have to go somewhere else to make copies, create a subcategory within your Errand file for photocopying.

## Read

For most of us, this is the biggest category, and everything you have to read will not fit in a file folder. (See the box on page 74 for more information on managing this category.)

## Sign

One of my clients used to complain that he spent too much time "on hold" on the telephone. His assistant complained that she couldn't get him to sign checks. By creating a red "Sign" file by his telephone, his assistant could get checks signed and he felt less frustrated about being on hold because he could accomplish something during the wait.

## Take Home (or Take to Work)

Designate a spot to put papers and other items you need to take home with you. Choose a convenient location—under the credenza, beside your briefcase, for example. If you are not accustomed to keeping your briefcase in the same spot all the time, try it—and have a similar setup at home.

## Write

Sometimes your "next action" will be to write a letter. This includes business letters, memos, thank you notes, and special occasion cards. If this is a problem area for you, take time to think about what you can do to make the task easier.

Certainly word-processing capability is an enormous asset for dealing with this task. For example, if you write a thank note in which you particularly like the words you used, and it fits a situation that's likely to arise again, file the letter in your computer under "Form Letters," in whatever subcategory seems appropriate, in this case, probably just "thank you's."

Other helpful hints:

- **Have note stationery on hand** so you can jot a quick personal note. A handwritten note is a very powerful tool in this technical, and frequently impersonal, age.

- **Keep various kinds of greeting cards on hand** for quick and effective communication.

- **Write a reply on the bottom of a letter** and fax the response.

- **If you're procrastinating about writing a letter, ask yourself if a phone call would do**—or have your assistant draft a response and you edit it.

- **Block out a specific time in your day for "Write."** Then check your "Write" files to determine which letters to write rather than noting each individual letter in your calendar.

- **Divide "write" into "personal" and "business" in manila folders.** I have a home office and I deal with both business and personal mail at my desk there. Having different folders allows for flexibility: When I am going to the doctor's office, for example, I often take "Write-personal" with me and jot a few notes to friends.

## Where to Put Your "Action" Files

**O**kay, now where do you *put* all these files? Well, it's a matter of preference, but accessibility is key. Some people prefer them on top of their desks or in a nearby file drawer. I use a combination system: I open the file drawer in my desk as soon as I sit down, so those files will be available for quick reference. Because my workstyle is to work on two or three major projects each day, I put those files in the "Hot Project" tray on top of my desk.

There are other ways to organize the folders you keep on your desktop:

- You can use manila (or your favorite color) files in a stairstep-type holder.

- There are a variety of attractive holders for hanging files that will sit on top of your desk or on a credenza.

- You could use a "hot file"—a plastic holder that hangs on the wall or on a file cabinet (if the holder has a magnetic back).

- Or there's the "Red Dot" System described in Chapter 12.

In any event, make sure that you can reach your "action" files—especially your most frequently used ones—from wherever you sit.

## Heeding Their Call

Now you may be wondering, "How will I remember to look in those files?" You don't have to remember—your calendar notations will remind you to look there at the appropriate time. Don't forget to use a symbol on your calendar (as described above and on the sample calendar on pages 60-61), to remind you to look. Besides, in many instances, such as with your "Call" file, there will be calls you'll automatically remember to make. When you check the file for information on those calls, you'll be reminded of the others you want to make.

You may be confused with the similarity between the purpose of your "To Do" list (Chapter 7) and your "action" files. Sometimes a "To Do" is just a thought, in which case you write it in your calendar or on your "To Do" list. Other times, a "To Do" involves a piece of paper that goes in the "action" file. An item noted on your "To Do" list and filed in your "action" file is not necessarily a duplication, unless you opt for a duplication system as an insurance policy, which many time management experts would recommend.

## Creating File Systems for Projects or Events

As I mentioned earlier, one method of sorting papers that require action is to divide them into categories by the name of a project or event (say, a trip or meeting). For example, as soon as I get the first piece of paper for an upcoming trip—a ticket, meeting announcement and so on—I create an "action" file for that trip. Here, I collect everything I plan to take with me, as well as reminders of things I want to pull from other files before I go. When the trip is over, I refile the information in the appropriate place.

Sometimes, when a project is very large, I create an entirely separate filing system of "reference" files and "action" files for that project.

For example, suppose you are thinking of undertaking a big project such as finding new building space. Instead of starting one file you know will be too small for the amount of material you'll collect, put whatever materials you have now in a pile on a bookshelf.

When you're ready to start the project, you can create your filing system for it. You may locate the project files in a section of your existing filing system, or you may set aside a separate drawer or container. If I have a paper-intensive temporary project, such as chairing a volunteer committee, I use a portable plastic filebox under my desk. It provides easy access and doesn't take up valuable file space from my regular filing system.

Categorize the materials into "action" files (for papers that require your action) and "reference" files (for papers you may need for future reference). You know the drill: "If I want this piece of paper again, what word will I think of?" ("reference" file) and "What's the next action I need to take on this piece of paper?" ("action" file) In some cases, you may have only one "reference" file and and one "action" file, while in a very large project, there may be many "reference" files and many "action" files.

## One CEO's "Action" File Method

This client keeps three basic "action" files, sorted by priority:

- **Urgent:** These are items he knows he has to do, and he handles them daily.
- **May be important:** He's not sure when he'll take care of these items, but if he hasn't heard from anyone in one month, he tosses them.
- **Probably not important:** If he hasn't heard from anyone in three months about these items, he tosses them.

Keep in mind that in an effective paper "flow" system, an "action" file can become a "reference" file and vice versa. An idea for a project that was in your "reference" files can become an action item, and thus, an "action" File. When the project is completed, it becomes a "reference" file once again. Or, you may create an "action" file at the beginning of the project that you will retire to the "reference" files once that phase of the project is over.

In my case, all project files are identified by the name of the client, whether it's a meeting planner, publisher, or a consulting client. It is an "action" file and contains everything related to that client, as long as the file is manageable. If the file gets too bulky to manage, I create a "reference" file for that client which contains the historical papers I want to keep.

## Applying Action Principles to E-Mail

Let's look at how we can apply this discussion of "action" files to the information you receive via your computer. (The best thing to do is reply to them as soon as possible!)

As with paper, consistency is the key to managing e-mail. To avoid letting an action slip through the cracks, you have three choices:

- **Print out and file** anything you want to keep in your paper system.

- **Copy or save to a file** anything you want to keep in your computer.

- **File in both systems.** You could have a paper file and a computer file on the same subject. Although this is an option, I don't think it's a terribly practical one. But if it works, and you like it, by all means do it.

### How it works for me

When I'm in the office, I generally check my e-mail first thing in the morning, at midday and before I leave the office. When I travel, I often only check at the end of each day.

As I read the message, I determine which of three actions—toss, answer or file—I plan to take:

- **If the action is "toss,"** I delete it immediately.

- **If I can't reply immediately because I don't know the answer or have the information I need,** I print out a copy of the message so I can keep track of it in my paper system. I then make a note in my calendar (if the action is required at a specific time) or on my "To Do" list (if it isn't), just as I would with a piece of paper that comes in my "In Box".

- **If I need to answer but don't have time or all the information I need at the moment,** I file the message in my "Out Box." My program reminds me I have messages in the "Out Box;" I **can't** forget to handle them.

- **If I send a message and want to make sure I get a reply,** I put a reminder in my calendar: "Heard from ___ re ___?"

- **If the e-mail message doesn't require action,** but I want to keep the information for future reference, I file it.

- **If the answer is "file" and a file exists,** I also do that immediately (to either a computer or paper file).

---

## Ready for Action at Barbara Hemphill's Desk

### Top of Desk
- **My calendar**
- **Phone message book** for recording voice-mail messages
- **"In Box"** for mail I haven't yet looked at
- **"In-Progress Box"** for my current "hot-project" "action" files
- **"Financial Box"** where I collect bills to pay
- **"Out Box"** for my assistant
- **"To File Box"** for items that will go to "reference" files

### Left Desk Drawer
"Action" files, including those for:
- **Call**
- **Calls waiting**
- **Computer entry**
- **Discuss**
- **Errands**
- **Pending,** with one file for each month
- **Write,** with one file each for business and personal correspondence

### Right Desk Drawer
"Action" files, including those for:
- **Projects and Upcoming Trips/Out-of Town**
- **Meetings,** filed in chronological order by the date of the trip
- **Current Clients,** a variety of project files that I file in alphabetical order

- **If I have to create a file** and I don't have time to think about it, I leave it in my e-mail and return to it later.

## Managing Your Voice Mail

Remember that consistency rule? It applies here, too. The first step to dealing effectively with your voice mail is to identify a place to record the contents of your messages. If your calendar or planner has enough writing space, you may choose to write them directly there—which is what I did for many years. My strategy changed as the number of calls increased and I gained an assistant who could help me return calls. Now, whoever listens to the message records it in a book on my desk and notes the initial of the person who is responsible for returning the call beside the message. As the message is acted upon or delivered to the appropriate person, it's crossed off the list.

The "Toss, Act, File" principle applies to voice mail just as it does to hard-copy paper and e-mail. Whenever possible, make a note of a message that you want to act upon in your calendar or your phone record book and delete the message right away. If the message should be handled by someone else, your voice-mail system may allow you to forward the message to their voice-mailbox, an alternative to my phone-record book strategy. Do so immediately.

Your voice-mail system may also allow you to "file" the message away in a so-called "archive" for future reference, for a certain number of days. There isn't much point to this unless you want to replay the message so someone else can literally "hear" it. Once there, the message is likely to expire without you acting on it.

If you want a record of a message that applies to a particular project, a better strategy is to write it on a separate piece of paper, with the date received, and file it in that project file.

**CHAPTER**

**9**

# Maintaining Your Files

**N**o matter how much time and energy you spend creating a system to fit your particular needs, you'll still need to adopt a plan to maintain the system. The following steps will help:

- **Continually Practice "The Art of Wastebasketry!"**
  Take steps to limit the amount of space you need for file storage. This is especially important in these days of modular offices, frequent office reorganizations, and computers, especially non-networked PCs.

- **Clean Out Whenever You Can**
  When you have a file in your hand or a directory on your computer screen, take an extra minute to eliminate whatever you know is unnecessary—even if it you can't do it perfectly. I can't count how many times I've seen a client holding something they *knew* they could toss stop and say, "I'll have to clean this out someday," and promptly put it back in the file instead of directly into the wastebasket. Perfectionism may have a place, but this isn't it!

- **Define Specific Retention Guidelines Whenever Possible**
  Put that information on the file index, or even on the file label itself. For example, "XYZ Newsletter—Keep 1 yr."

- **Determine Who Will Do the Filing and When**
  If the filing system is well-designed, even temporary employees who know little about your business can actually do the filing. If you are the only one to do it, make an appointment with yourself to do it—every Friday or when the "To File Box" gets full.

- **Establish an annual "File Clean Out Day"**
  Choose a time when your work schedule is likely to be less hectic—around the holidays, for example. For the self-employed person, try just after tax time, when you're still familiar with your files but not overwhelmed with tax preparation.

  Or you could just wait until you need the file space. As long as you have room to file papers easily, purging isn't a major issue. But when you neglect filing the paper you would like to file, because it's downright impossible to get your fingers into the file cabinet, or you spend precious time scrolling up and down your computer screen looking for a file, then it's time for Clean Out Day! (See Chapter 16.)

## The Importance of the File Index

After you've completed your File Index, make sure that it remains a "living document." Make notations on your printed copy when you add or delete a file, and then periodically update the Index in your computer and print out clean copies. If you make an Index and then put it in a drawer and forget about it, you're very likely to forget the file titles you chose, and make a file for "Personnel" when you already have "Employees." If *that* happens, you'll be back to where you started in no time.

## Stumbling Blocks to Success

Few people enjoy filing, and most of us procrastinate, sometimes for a long time. Even people who are paid to file sometimes let their "To File Box" overflow! Those who should know better delay creating and assigning appropriate places to file their computer files.

Why? Well:

- **Sometimes, you just don't *want* to file!**
  The consequences may not be so bad when you're dealing with paper—chances are you have an idea of

*Remember, filing something will never be any easier than it is today, and every day you wait it becomes more difficult!*

which pile to look in if you need something. But on your computer, if you don't actively decide where to file something when you save it, your computer will make the decision for you and file it in the last place you were working. The result is a misfiled document that'll be really hard to find again if you have any quantity of files on your system. Say you write a memo about office reorganization, but you save it in a directory related to new business. Next time you look for the computer copy of the memo, you probably won't have a clue where to find it, and you'll have to waste precious time hunting through your many directories. (And that assumes you gave your memo a file name that you'll recognize!)

"I think I've discovered the bottleneck."

*Farris, Cartoonists & Writers Syndicate*

- **Filing can be time-consuming.**
  This is particularly true if the filing system is poorly organized and you've let a lot of stuff accumulate. Many people give up, and just leave those piles of paper in a box to deal with "later." (Which, believe it or not, may be the best strategy—see the discussion of dealing with your backlog on page 24.) Some even leave a multitude of electronic project files—working drafts, final versions, memos, tables, and so on—languishing in their computers, hidden behind file names that made sense when being used, but that have become mysterious with time. Remember, filing something will never be any easier than it is today, and every day you wait it becomes more difficult!

- **You may not know how to file things so you can find them again.**

  That might help explain the first two stumbling blocks, too. Reading this book will solve that problem!

  Remember, "No job is finished until the paperwork is done." After you've finished the "fun" part of a project, a meeting, or a trip, you've got to cope with the information you've accumulated. You'll find that you'll be more willing to file—and it will take less time—when you know how. The results of having a filing system that works are positive *and* long-lasting—and well worth the effort!

*CATHY © Cathy Guisewite. Reprinted with permission of Universal Press Syndicate. All Rights Reserved.*

# Organizing
# Your Computer

In addition to organizing the paper which results from our new technology, we now also have to organize the technology itself. Luckily, the principles are the same as those we've already discussed in the book. Now lets look at how to apply them.

Fortunately, with the advent of Windows 95, all computer users now have the advantages that Macintosh users have had for years when it comes to organization. The combination of the 255-character file name plus the search capability gives us access to a powerful organizing tool.

## How Computer Filing Works

Your computer is basically an electronic filing cabinet. This is true regardless of what kind of operating system your computer uses, what kind of graphical interface it uses to show you how things are organized, what tools are available to you, and what kind of words or icons it uses to identify and describe those features.

Whether you use an IBM compatible or Macintosh, the principles of organizing the programs and the information in them are basically the same. What *does* matter, to some extent, is the way the operating system shows you the file index that your computer generates and how it allows you to manipulate it. If you have installed Windows on your IBM compatible, you have most of the same user-friendly file management features that a Macintosh user enjoys. I'll discuss more about these features later in the chapter.

Bottom-line, your computer-filing system can be set

*(continued on page 88)*

## Your Computer: An Electronic File Cabinet

| PAPER | COMPUTER |
|---|---|
| **Filing cabinet for storing information** | **Hard disk.** This is where you store your documents and your com puter programs. The computer reads or accesses the information on the hard disk via the drive, just like playing a CD on a CD player. |
| **Brief case** | **"Removable medium"** which includes a 3 ½" diskette, a 5 ¼" diskette, CD-ROM, or a removable cartridge. Your computer has an A: drive, the slot on the front of the computer where you can insert and run a floppy disk, and may have additional drives. |
| **Multiple filing cabinets** | **Local area network (LAN).** If your personal computer or Macintosh is "networked," this means that your computer and all of the other computers on the system are connected to multiple drives in various locations in order to share disk drives and other com-ponents, such as printers, fax modems, tape back-ups, etc. |
| **File drawer** | **File directory.** This is where you keep all files in a single category. For example, you could keep all files related to your word pro-cessing program in one file directory, or all files related to a major project, client, etc. in another directory. *Note:* File directo-ries and subdirectories (see below) in DOS and Windows are the equivalent of "folders" in Macintosh. |
| **Hanging file** | **File subdirectory.** This is where you keep all files related to a single subcategory of the larger file directory. For example, the directo-ry might be CLIENTX, while the subdirectory would be CLIEN-TX/LETTERS. If multiple people are using the same computer, you could have a directory for each user, who would in turn cre-ate subdirectories for their projects. You can create subdirectories several layers deep. For example: CLIENTX/LETTERS/ SMITH/CAMPAIGN. |
| **Manila file** | **Computer file.** This is where you keep a document or all documents related to a single subcategory of the subdirectory. |
| **File label** | **File name.** |
| **Piece of paper** | **File (word processing document, spread sheet, presentation, etc.).** |
| **File index** | **The Windows Explorer, File Manager, and the Macintosh Desktop.** These are visual ways of seeing all the programs that you have in your computer. |

up very similarly to your paper-filing system. The box on page 87 shows how.

# Setting Up Your Computer-Filing System

If you have a computer full of files, and you spend more time than you can afford looking for files, the easiest way to get yourself out of the quagmire is to start over—just as we discussed for your paper-filing system. What does that mean? Ignore all your old files. Design your new computer-filing system, using the principles we are going to discuss. Then refile the old files into the new system as you need them or, whenever possible, delete them.

How do you design an effective computer-filing system? Well, for one thing, you must remember one of the most important (and most neglected) principles of organizing computer files: A computer's value is that it allows you to use a file again. Sometimes you may simply want to print another copy of the document. Other times, you may want to update or change the document in some way. But if you don't intend to use the document again, there's no value in storing it in a computer. If you need to keep a copy of a file for reference, your alternatives are to keep a hard copy in your paper-filing system or a copy on a disk for the purposes of archiving.

## *Organizing the "Keepers"*

The first step to effectively organizing your computer is to point all files into one directory, regardless of what program created those files. (It's the same principle as filing paper information according to how you will use it, not where you got it.) I call it "Files"—others call it "Data," or you may have another term.

This will make it easier to retrieve what you need, regardless of what program created it, and make it easier to back it up for archives or for transfer to other locations.

It's been my experience that in paper systems, people frequently get into trouble because they have too many categories, while in computer systems, they get into trouble because they have too *few* categories (i.e., directories and subdirectories).

Why are the two systems different? Because it's easier to flip through one file that has 20 pieces of paper in it than it is to go through 10 files with two pieces of paper in each. On the other hand, it's easier to scroll up and down a computer screen looking for directories and subdirectories than to open documents. In addition, your computer gives you a "search" capability that will help you find the file you want by searching for key words without having to actually open each file. Of course, you can ignore the option of creating subdirectories and keep all your files in one directory, but that would be like tossing all your tools in your garage and then spending hours looking for a screwdriver!

## *Categories That Reflect Your Work*

The next step is to determine the major categories of your files. Those might include: project or client names, geographical locations, or even your professional and personal roles, if you wear different hats when using your computer.

For example, I have a directory for my first book entitled "Taming1," with subdirectories for each chapter, as well as for book-related issues, such as marketing materials and pricing information. I call the directory for my role as a board member of the Carolina Speaker's Association simply "CSA." Because I keep very few documents related to CSA, I do not have a subdirectory for it. I've entitled another directory "Clients," for materials I've created for my clients. Each client has a subdirectory.

Some of my favorite directories are:

1. **Pending:** For files on which you're currently working. You can quickly see which documents are in process, or if necessary, it will be easy for someone else to retrieve your work.

2. **Out Box:** Here you can file work which you've completed, but need to print, fax, give to someone else, or send to another location when you have access to a modem.

*File all your data on a removable cartridge instead of on your hard drive, so that you can carry them with you. This ensures that you will always have all the files you need when and where you need them!*

3. **Home:** For information you need to take home with you.

4. **Office:** For information you need to take to the office.

## Which Drive is the Right One?

If you're working on a networked computer, you may have a choice of multiple drives in which to file your documents. Your organization may already have made this decision of which drive to use for you. For example, all files of mutual business interest or used by a single division of the business may be filed on one drive, while employees' private work files may be filed on another.

Whatever you do, don't make your strategy too complicated. It would, for example, probably be more confusing than helpful to send five separate projects to five separate drives, when there's space for all of them on the same drive, especially if they're all related to the same role or client in your work life.

# Naming Your Files

### Working within the limits of space

If you are using DOS or a pre-Windows '95 program, you're limited in naming your computer file to eight characters plus an extension of three characters.

Most programs automatically assign the 3-character extension. In some programs, you can change the three letters for better identification. In WordPerfect, for example, you can use the character extension to help identify the file, such as "LTR" for letter, while in Microsoft Word the extension is automatically ".doc" or ".dot." You may not use punctuation marks, certain symbols or spaces in file names.

If your program only allows 8 characters, you can purchase a program (Long File Names) which gives you the ability to use file names that are longer and make more sense. In Word, you can use the "Summary" feature, which allows you to list additional information and key words to help you find the file.

### What word will I think of first?

To determine how to name a file, use the same technique we discussed for paper files: Ask yourself, "If I want this file again, what word will I think of first?" Enter that word first, and then any other word which might help you retrieve that file. Separate the identifying words with commas. For example, project for clients might be filed in a "Client" directory as: SMITH ASSOCIATES, Bill Smith, Brown, recycling, aluminum, Seattle; or

RUBBERMAID, promotion, spokesperson, media, Knoxville, Autodesk, HGTV;

USA TODAY, advertorial, spokesperson, marketing, Destinations, Mark Brown.

## Coordinating Your Computer Files and Your Paper Files

It's not necessary to have a paper file for every computer file (especially not as a way to back up your computer), and vice versa. But I've found that it's often advantageous to use a system in your computer files that reflects the system you use in your paper files, especially if you expect to *use* the two forms of material together. For example, in my computer I have a subdirectory entitled C:\FILES\PROMO\SEMINARS. "C:\" is my computer's hard drive, and "Files" is the directory where I store all my data. But more to the point, "Promo" is the directory I use for all promotional material used by my company, and "Seminars" is the subdirectory that I use for promotional material for seminars. The folder name indicates the specific seminar, such as ASAE, Chicago, Dec95, Auction, Cindy Smith, Taming.

I also have a paper file entitled "Promotion-Seminars" which contains the individual outlines I use for each seminar. Each outline in the paper file has a notation in the upper right-hand corner identifying the actual document name in the computer.

That way, if a meeting planner calls and says, "I'd like to see an outline for a three-hour program on time management," I can use my hard-copy file to look at several outlines

**Software Installation**

*Install new software programs one at a time. If you install several at once, and there's a defect in one of the programs, it will be difficult to determine which program caused the problem.*

at once. And I can then easily create a new document on my computer by copying paragraphs from whichever outlines I choose to suit the need of my client or prospective client.

## Tracking Your Work Without Keeping Computer Copies of Everything

When I return from a business trip I usually have several thank you letters to write. I see no value in storing those letters in my computer, nor do I want to clutter up

### Comparing Your Filing Options: Paper and Computer

So let's create a document in paper and on the computer. Say, for example, you want to write a memo to your boss about developing a new brochure, and you want to keep a copy for your files.

#### The Paper-Filing World

**Creating the memo:** You pull out a blank sheet of paper and handwrite or type the text of your memo, send the original and keep a copy for your files.

Or, you write the memo in your word-processing program, print two copies—one to send and one to file—and don't bother to save the document on the computer.

**What you might do:** You toss your copy of the memo in your "To File" box.

#### The Computer-Filing World

**Creating the memo:** You open up your word-processing program and type your memo on the blank screen presented to you for a new document. You print out one copy to send and keep a copy in the computer for future reference.

**What you might do:** In a rush, you tell the program to save and close the document, but don't bother to name it yourself. Your word-processing program does the job for you, naming the document something meaningless like "doc2.doc," (which only happens in Word) which means this is the second document you've neglected to name in this program (The doc following the 2 is the three-letter "extension" that identifies the type of document, that is, the program in which you created it.) *Note:* Some programs, such as Word Perfect, will not allow you to close a document without giving it a specific file name.

my paper files with thank you notes.

To solve this problem, I have a "chron" file (or pile, if you prefer) which contains copies—filed chronologically—of every letter I print. Then if I suddenly wonder, "Did I actually write that thank you to Ms. Forrest, or did I just think about it?" I can easily check. This way I haven't cluttered up my paper files or my computer—and I can purge the chron file after a year. (Of course, if the letter contained information I want to keep, I'd file it in the client file.)

If you use a contact-manager program, such as ACT!,

### The Paper-Filing World

**What happens next:** You need your copy of the memo and you must go digging through your "To File" box to find it.

**The better way:** At this point of filing your copy, ask yourself, "If I want this piece of paper again, what word will I think of first?" Check your File Index to see if that file exists. If not, add it to the list. Note that word in the upper right-hand corner of your copy of the memo, so you, or the person who does your filing, will know where to file it.

Because you'll work on more than one publication at a time, you designate space in one of your file drawers for Publications and add it to the label on the outside of the file drawer. You create a hanging file, "Publication - XYZ," for the current brochure that you're working on.

As you create other documents related to the XYZ brochure, you add them to the front of the existing file in the order they are sent. If the file becomes too thick to manage, you subdivide the file into smaller categories such as "XYZ-Price Estimates" and "XYZ-Proofs."

### The Computer-Filing World

**What happens next:** You need your copy of the memo and you must scrounge through your file directory, looking for a file name that rings a bell. Completely ignoring those anonymous doc.docs, you give up!

**The better way:** When you're done writing any document, you save it by deciding (1) which drive to keep it on, if you have more than one option, and then, (2) which directory or subdirectory. Then you name the file by asking "If I want this information again, what word will I think of first?"

You create a directory called PUBS, with a subdirectory/XYZ, and save your new document to: PUBS/XYZ.doc. You "save the new document to" (that is, file it in) the subdirectory Pubs/XYZ.

You can reorganize files into new directories or subdirectories by using the "drag and drop" feature or the "move" command.

MAXIMIZER, SHARKWARE, etc., (see page 49), another option would simply be to make a note in the client's computer file that you had sent a thank you note.

Suppose you write a thank you note that you particularly like and might want to use its wording in future thank you letters? Refile it in your computer directory/subdirectory called: Forms/Thankyou.

"I don't suppose you'd consider using a filebox?"

*Toos, Cartoonists & Writers Syndicate*

## Maintaining Your Computer Filing System

**U**nlike the file index for your file cabinets, your computer file index is automatically generated for you and updates itself every time you create a new file, directory or subdirectory. However, it's still a good idea to revisit your computer file index periodically to see if it still reflects your needs.

### Cleaning Out

Keeping your hard drive free of unwanted files is a good idea, especially for people who have laptops and smaller disk drives.

You can delete files that contain documents you know you will not need again. Those might include:

- Working drafts of documents that have since been completed.

- Empty files that you created but never did anything with (or that you moved material out of).

- Files by different names that contain duplicate material.

- Files that are too old to be reused.

One note of caution: Removing program-type files can wreak havoc with your computer. If the software writes the file, do not touch it—even a .BAK file.

You can copy all files that you want to keep for reference to disks, which you can organize using the suggestions given beginning on page 99. Although the file index in Windows or on the Macintosh would typically be alphabetized by file name, you can alternatively specify that they be sorted by type (that is, by the file extension), size (amount of computer memory taken up), or—most importantly for our purposes here—by the date that it was created or last worked on. So you could, for example, sort by date and review only those files last revised six months ago or longer. You could then copy those files that you wanted to save for reference to floppy disks and delete the rest from the hard disk.

If your computer is networked, storage capacity may not be an issue. If it is, chances are your network's system manager will have to monitor the network's capacity and will initiate a company computer-file clean-out day if the system is approaching its limits.

## Preventing Disaster: Backing Up Your Computer

Can you imagine what would happen if some very strong person up-ended your filing cabinet so that all your files and papers fell in a heap on the floor? Your papers could end up scrambled beyond recognition, or some of them could slide under the furniture and you'd never find them again. While this is only remotely possible with your file cabinets, it's far more likely with your computer. If a hard disk crashes, you could lose months' worth of work or only partially recover it—to say nothing of what it would do to your blood pressure!

In most cases, it's only a matter of time before your computer crashes. Therefore, backing up the information on it is an *essential* organizing task. Some people copy all their files from the hard disk to a bunch of floppy disks. Although backup programs make this task easier, it's still a time-consuming chore. Who wants to spend half an hour backing up computer files after finishing work? The best way to do this is with a high capacity removable tape back-up unit (such as SyQuest or Berneulli) and a good back-up software (such as Colorado or Arcadia). In addition, a compression program (such as Stacker or DriveSpace, which is built into Windows 95) will require less space to back up your files.

Backing up is easy enough to do, but like all organizing tasks, you have to remember to do it—*regularly*. How often is "often enough" depends on how much you value your time and how critical the work is that you are doing. Once a week might be enough for some folks, but if you're working on a critical project where mere hours count, then you might want to back up those project files every few hours. A removable system can automatically and easily do a daily back-up.

You can also tell the computer to do a modified back-up—only those documents that have changed since the last time you backed up.

## *Tape Rotation Back-Up System*

The key to protecting your data is routine backup and tape rotation (or whatever medium you are using) to ensure you can restore selected files or an entire disk as needed. How you back up depends on the number of daily changes you make and your need for historical data.

No matter which method you choose, you should always have at least two sets of tapes and alternate using them, so if one set is damaged, the other is available.

---

## *Three Back-up Methods*

• • • • • • • • • • • • • • • • • • • • • • •

1. **Total**—saves all files and directories on the drive you specify.

2. **Selective**—you choose specific files and directories to back up. Selection is possible at any level: directories, subdirectories or individual files. With this option it's simple to transfer data to other sites or archive selected files for storage.

3. **Modified**—Backs up only files that have been changed since your last backup.

Here are other options:

- **Three-tape Rotation:** Designed for users whose files don't change very much on a daily basis:

| | | |
|---|---|---|
| Tape 1 | Monday | Total Backup |
| Tape 2 | Tues, Wed, Thurs. | Modified Backup |
| Tape 3 | Friday | Total Backup |

- **Six-tape Rotation:** A tape for each workday and one to store off-site is an easy method to keep a recent copy of our data files on hand at all times (my preference).

| | | |
|---|---|---|
| Tape 1 | Monday | Total Backup |
| Tape 2 | Tuesday | Modified Backup |
| Tape 3 | Wednesday | Modified Backup |
| Tape 4 | Thursday | Modified Backup |
| Tape 5 | Friday | Modified Backup |
| Tape 6 | Off Site | Total Backup |

- **Ten-tape Rotation:** Designed for users who need to preserve months of data and need a historical record of their work.

| | | |
|---|---|---|
| Tape 1 | Monday | Total Backup |
| Tape 2 | Tuesday | Modified Backup |
| Tape 3 | Wednesday | Modified Backup |
| Tape 4 | Thursday | Modified Backup |
| Tape 5 | Friday | Modified Backup |
| Tape 6 | Off Site | Total Backup |
| Tape 7 | Week 2 | Total Backup |
| Tape 8 | Week 3 | Total Backup |
| Tape 9 | Week 4 | Total Backup |
| Tape 10 | Month Total | Total Backup |

**The Backup Tape Label**

First, label tapes in pen with the user's name and the day of the week (for 5 tapes) and "Off Site" (for tape #6). Second, fill in the tape number and date in pencil so you can erase it the next time you use that series of tapes.

Here's a sample of the label from my back-up tape:

> *H + A BACKUP — MONDAY*
> Tape # __1__ of __5__ Date: __10/30/95__

It's wise to keep a file of all the original software disks for the computer programs you use. That way, if your computer crashes, you can easily re-install the programs you need. Even if your computer comes with programs already installed on the hard disk, you should still receive original disks or be able to make back-up copies yourself from the program. Keep your back-up off-site or in a fireproof safe.

## *Three Reasons for a Tape Back-up*

• • • • • • • • • • • • • • • • • • • • • • •

1. **Protect against data loss**—If a data loss occurs, simply restore your data, eliminating the need to rekey and reconstruct.

2. **Archive data**—It provides an effective method for storing seldom-used files and for long-term storage. It also allows you to easily transfer data between home and work.

3. **Increase system performance**—Performing a total disk backup, erasing the disk, and restoring from tape to disk reduces file fragmentation, which increases speed. You can also increase system performance by storing data that you do not use regularly off-line. The system can then access information more quickly since it does not have to read through as many files on your hard drive.

### If you're on a network

If your computer is networked, you probably don't have to worry about backing up your files for safekeeping. That's because most networks are backed up regularly by the system administrator or automatically by the network itself. But before you assume this is the case, check with your system administrator to find out about your company's back-up practices. You'll want to know the following:

- **How often is the system backed up?** If it's backed up every other day, are you willing to lose two days' work?

- **If the system crashes, how long would it be before you'd again have access to the documents you need?** A few hours may not be a problem, but a day or two when you're on deadline may be a big problem. In which case, again, you need to be backing up your critical files yourself on a local tape .

- **Which of the programs that you use are installed for everyone's benefit on the network?** Which programs are installed "locally" in your computer and wouldn't automatically be reinstalled on the network after a system crashed? Be sure to keep backup copies of those programs.

### *Avoid the Tomb of the Unknown*

Ever had one of those exasperating moments when you need something and realize that you've got to search through a pile of outdated, mislabeled, unidentified and disorganized disks or tapes to find it?

As with many organizing tasks, the solution isn't complicated—it just requires consistency. It'll be much easier to retrieve information if you use that basic organizing principle, "Put like things together."

For starters, put all your program disks together in one container and all your backup disks in another. (It is easier to retrieve disks from one large container rather than several small ones.)

If you are using CDs, you can save space by throwing away the jewel cases they come in, and store them in cases. A zipper case holds 100 CDs and is great for traveling.

On disks or tapes, label with non-smear markers for permanent labels, or with pencil for information that will change, such as a date.

Identify a specific location where you can collect disks or tapes that you can reuse.

## *Whenever you purchase new software*

• • • • • • • • • • • • • • • • • • • • • • • • •

- Put all software diskettes in one place.

- Register the software according to the manual.

- Determine what customer support is available, and make sure to record your customer number whenever one is assigned, e.g., in your card file.

- If you no longer use an outdated software program, remove it from your computer, and discard the manuals and support information from your office.

## *Preserving Your Privacy*

*DILBERT reprinted by permission of United Features Syndicate, Inc.*

It's unlikely that people would walk in and nose around in the file cabinets in your office. If they were, you could probably keep them out with a simple lock on the file cabinet. Similarly, if you keep top secret or personal files on your computer, share a computer with someone (including a home computer that you work on and other family members play on), or if your computer is networked, you might want to give some files special passwords.

If you password any of your files, don't take chances on committing the passwords to memory. It's a big time-waster and source of frustration to try to open a file and realize that you can't remember the password.

# A Note About Groupware (Project-Management Software)

Lotus Notes is the most famous software in a relatively new category of products known as groupware. Simply stated, groupware allows individual computer users to be a part of a group and share information. This software can help you do the following:

- Create databases, and specify who sees the information. This can be one person, everyone in a department or the entire company.

- Make sure that all company forms are standard. All company forms will be on-line, which will make you look much more organized.

- All information can be backed up and kept safe.

- Confidential information is kept on-line so that it's more difficult to get to than having papers on everyone's desk.

- Information can be derived from many different sources and kept in Lotus Notes.

- All of the most popular operating systems are supported, making communications very easy. Lotus Notes supports Microsoft Windows, Apple Macintosh, IBM OS/2, and Unix.

- Reduce the barriers of geography. All employees can be connected and share in discussions, news, access vital corporate data, etc., regardless of their location.

What makes Lotus Notes so powerful is that it becomes a central repository for information that the company wants to keep and use on an ongoing basis. The software can be used for reference, workflow, e-mail, and fax. It has excellent formatting and searching capabilities. The software not only handles internal company communications well but also facilitates communications to the outside world through e-mail and fax.

As a holding tank for the vital information of the organization, groupware has many uses. Some companies use Lotus Notes to keep all of their documents on-line and current. Others develop superior products by organizing engineering, marketing, sales, administration, and manufacturing departments on Lotus Notes. This reduces the number of meetings and provides better communications between departments as the project progresses.

Because of its sophisticated features, Lotus Notes has quickly become the standard by which all groupware products are measured. Groupware has become a popular way for companies to get more organized. These products, when implemented properly, can help the organization use the various information collected every day and reach its objectives easier.

# THREE

# Organizing In Special Situations

# When You Work from Home

**A**n increasing number of people are discovering the pleasures—and challenges—of working in a home office. According to Link Resources, a market-research firm in New York City, nearly 60 million Americans will be working at home by 1998. Most are entrepreneurs, but the greatest growth is a result of telecommunicators who are based at home while working for a company.

## *Take It From One Who Knows*

When you work at home, often the biggest challenge in staying organized and managing your time is convincing others that you're working! Assertive behavior is essential. If a friend calls to chat about personal business at 10:00 a.m., politely say, "I'm in the middle of a work project right now. May I call you this evening?" In the case of children, explain what you are doing as clearly as you can and establish some physical sign to indicate when you are working and not to be disturbed except in emergencies. A closed door works wonders!

Don't try to be a supervising parent and a professional at the same time. Consider hiring a teenage neighbor or senior citizen to provide day care, whether in your home or theirs. (Consult your accountant about any possible tax implications.) Make a commitment to spend specific time with your children. Be sure to honor your promise.

## *A Real Office For Real Work*

Just having a home office isn't enough to guarantee that you'll get work done there. If you haven't designed your space to suit your needs and your personality, with the right tools in the right places, your productivity and peace of mind will suffer. Obviously, many of the decisions you make regarding your home office will be based on finances, but even if yours are limited there are numerous possibilities.

### Consider your comfort

The first step is to choose a comfortable place to work, and most importantly, a place you *like* to be. If you like sunshine or have allergies to mold, the basement is probably not a viable choice. I was once hired by a woman who had a beautiful custom-built home—including a well-designed office that, she reluctantly admitted, she rarely used. When I walked into her home, I immediately understood why. The dining room table (where her papers were spread) was in front of a window that overlooked a beautiful lake—while the view from her desk was a cluttered bulletin board.

### Pay attention to your furniture

The roll-top desk you inherited from your grandfather may be gorgeous, but if you have difficulty keeping track of papers in it, or don't have room for your computer and keyboard, it could spell disaster. Furniture that is functional and comfortable is essential. Your desk is crucial to your work. For most people, the bigger, the better. An L-shape is preferable for using a computer or typewriter. Most people find it easier to organize their work area if the desk has *at least* one file drawer.

### Good-quality filing cabinets are essential

Two-drawer lateral files that create counter space for equipment such as a photocopier and fax machine are often very practical. One client who used her dining room for an office purchased beautiful wooden filing cabinets that matched her Scandinavian furniture and could be used as a side table for serving food when she had guests.

If your home office area is too small to accommodate all the file cabinets you need, put them in some other location in the house, and put a "To File" box on or near your desk to gather papers that you'll take to that location.

As a last resort, consider off-site storage, but only for those reference files that you are least likely to use any time soon. You don't want to run down to the storage center very often. Besides, if those files are expendable enough that you'd consider placing them in off-site storage, think about disposing of them, un-less they have long-term tax or other legal implications. By all means, avoid using an off-site location to store postponed decisions! Make sure that storage space is worth what it costs you.

"I've been watching you, Leachkin. You seem to really like your computer. You're giving the rest of us the willies."

*Toos, Cartoonists & Writers Syndicate*

## Phoning from home

Having enough telephone lines and selecting the right equipment is also an important issue. Although technology now makes it possible to use one phone line in a variety of ways, such as different rings for different recipients, fax machines, and on-line services, it is often not practical to do so.

I recommend a minimum of two lines—one for personal use and one for business. You can use your personal line for outgoing calls so you don't tie up your business line for customers trying to reach you, and you can put your fax machine on your personal line.

Many people who have a home office need more than one business line—particularly if clients call frequently. To determine how many lines you really need, consider how many phone-related activities might happen at once:

- Is there likely to be more than one person in your office at the same time?

- Do you have a separate fax machine or an internal fax on your computer?

- Do you use on-line services? Frequently? For extended periods of time?

When selecting telephone equipment, you may find cordless phones convenient, but make sure you don't sacrifice quality of sound. Aside from your need to communicate easily and well, you don't want to give your clients the impression that when working at home, you're working second-rate.

### No need to miss messages

One major "phone issue" is call coverage—what happens if you can't answer the phone and there's no one to back you up. The obvious solution is a separate "business" answering machine. If you travel or are out of the office frequently, be sure to select one that has a "remote" feature that allows you to check your incoming messages and change your outgoing message from an off-site location.

Another option is to choose a voice mail service provided by your telephone company (look under "Business Services" in your local telephone directory) or a separate company (look under "Telephone Answering Service" in the Yellow Pages).

In addition to your regular number, you may wish to use an "800" number assigned to a separate telephone line,

---

## *Seven Most Common Home Office Mistakes*

• • • • • • • • • • • • • • • • • • • • • • • •

- Wrong location
- Lack of dedicated space
- Inappropriate furniture and equipment
- Lack of filing space
- A filing system that doesn't work
- Shortage of book and storage space
- An excess of clutter

---

so you can track calls you receive. For a few additional dollars a month, you can have the 800 number ring right on your regular line.

# Home-Office Equipment Basics

## *Your Computer*

In this day and age, a home office without a computer would be rather like a car without an engine! That doesn't necessarily mean that you have to have the latest and greatest. That would be an endless game, because it's nearly impossible to keep pace with technological advances.

However, don't do yourself a disservice in the long run so you can save money in the short run. Whatever computer you purchase should have enough memory and speed to run the software that you need to do your job efficiently. And it's smart to purchase the most equipment you can afford so you can keep up with new versions of your software without having to purchase every new generation of hardware.

To determine what you really need, first identify what kind of activities are important to you and where you'll do them:

## When Your Office Moves

If you move and you can't move your telephone number to your new location, consider these two options:

- Arrange for the telephone company to have calls to your old number forwarded directly to your new number, or

- Put your old number directly into a voice mail box, and check it daily.

Through the wonders of technology I have kept the same telephone number for 17 years, even though I have had a home office in six locations in two states. When I first started my business in Virginia, I didn't have anyone to answer my phone when I was out. I also wanted a Washington, D.C. telephone number, so I used a Washington, D.C. phone answering service. When I hired someone to work in my office and answer my phone, I put that number directly on call forwarding into my Virginia home office. The caller thought they were talking to someone in Washington, D.C., but in fact, we were in Virginia. Several years later, I moved to North Carolina, but wanted to keep my Washington, D.C. "presence," so I put that number into a voice mail box, which I check daily.

- **If you do most of your work in the office,** a desktop computer will be fine.

- **If you do most of your work outside the office,** or you want to be able to work in other locations, you may need a portable computer.

- **If someone else will be working in your office,** you may need more than one computer.

- **Identify the software that's critical to your work** and make sure that whatever computer you choose will accommodate it and allow you to work efficiently.

Then the question is whether your computers need to be networked. Do they need to talk to each other, or can you use each computer for specific activities, and transfer information from one computer to another by disk when necessary. For example, I have three computers in my office: a desktop computer on my desk, used primarily for word processing and desktop publishing, a desktop at my assistant's desk, used primarily for accounting activities and database management, and a notebook computer I carry with me, used primarily for writing.

Keep in mind that the purchase of the machine is a small percentage of the actual costs of a computer. You also have to include the cost of the software and other

## 10 Questions to Ask Before Buying Office Equipment

- What is my primary incentive for buying this equipment? What will I be able to do that I can't do now?

- Will it "pay" in terms of increased productivity or reduced stress?

- Can I afford not to have it, or will others interpret my failure to have this equipment as lack of professionalism?

- Do I need it because it is going to become the standard that everyone expects?

- Is there a cheaper way to accomplish the same thing?

- Would it be more cost-effective to lease the equipment?

- Is the equipment "fast" enough—or more than I need or can afford?

- Do I have the physical space the equipment requires?

- How will I learn to use the equipment?

- What additional services do I want or need with this equipment—maintenance contract, additional telephone lines, training or consulting services?

equipment you may need, as well as costs incurred in setting up and learning the system. Although you may be able to do that by using books and manuals, you may find it easier (and cheaper in the long run) to hire a consultant. He or she can help you purchase and set up a system that meets your needs, provide you with training, propose and install upgrades when appropriate, troubleshoot and just generally help you avoid a lot of personal and professional teeth-grinding.

## Fax Machines

Because I send and receive several faxes per day, I prefer a freestanding fax machine with a "dedicated" line. I purchased a fax machine with a telephone handset, so I can use it as an additional telephone if I have to. If most of the faxes you send will be created on your computer, a modem and a fax software package may be all you need. I use both methods.

## A Copy Machine

The first piece of office equipment I purchased was a copy machine—and I've *never* been sorry. One of my favorite networking activities is sending copies of favorite articles, with my business card and/or a short note attached, to clients or potential clients. My photocopy machine makes that a snap.

Multiple function machines can combine all or some of the above activities.

## The Alternative: Office Support Services

This is one of the fastest-growing industries today. This can include everything from renting office space in a building with many other offices, with answering services, mail rooms, conference rooms, and a variety of equipment at your disposal. There are also companies where you can rent a post office box, use printing and mailing services, and rent equipment such as computers and printers by the hour.

### Don't Skimp On Supplies

Be sure to have all the office supplies you need. A quick recipe for panic—and increased cost—is discovering that you're out of letterhead in the middle of printing a major proposal. Always have on hand extra toner cartridges for printers and copy machines. Keep a running shopping list for supplies you need to purchase—make a note when you use the *next to the last* roll of fax paper, so you don't have to make emergency shopping trips. Keep the list in an easily accessible place, such as your "Errands" action file, or posted inside the supply closet door. Make sure anyone else who works in your office knows where it is—and uses it!

### Don't Get Clobbered By The Personal Touch

An excess of clutter can be a problem in any office, but it's more tempting at home—particularly if you're a "keeper" and short on space! I'm not suggesting a pristine environment makes a *better* work space, but many people have too much "stuff" in the areas where they're trying to work. Memorabilia can become distracting when there's too much of it. Identify a particular place for memorabilia in your office. When that place becomes full, it's time to make decisions: toss it, move it, or put in storage.

---

## *Resources for Home-Based Businesses*

• • • • • • • • • • • • • • • • • • • • • • •

*Home Office Computing* (P.O. Box 2511, Boulder, CO 80302; $19.97 per year) provides valuable information in a very readable style about issues affecting people who work out of their homes.

*Working Solo Sourcebook* by Terri Lonier ($14.95) and *Working Solo Newsletter* ($24 for a one-year subscription of four issues; $4 for a sample issue) from Portico Press, PO Box 190, New Paltz, NY 12561-0190; 800–222–7656.

*What to Buy for Business: The Independent Consumer Guide to Business Equipment* (What to Buy For Business Inc., 924 Anacapa Street, Suite 4G, Santa Barbara, CA 93101; 800-247-2185; $121 for a subscription of ten issues, including any updates; $23 per single issue, plus $3 for shipping and handling).

---

# Working on the Road

Just because you're on the road doesn't mean that you can't take care of business as usual—if you have the right tools. I find my travel time to be my most productive because I'm less distracted by phone calls and other interruptions. I find new places and things inspiring, so travel time is the best time for me to work on projects that require creativity and concentration. And sometimes, "productive" means catching up on some much-needed rest!

## Equipment to Consider

### Start With The Phone

Most business people have cellular phones installed in their cars, or carry portable cellular phones. One of the biggest joys of my portable phone is not having to search frantically for a pay phone and dig in my handbag for loose change. (But if there *is* a pay phone handy, and I have loose change available, I use it, because it's less expensive.)

If you use a portable phone because you want other people to reach you there, you'll also need a voice mail system to catch calls that you're not able to answer. You can purchase voice mail from the cellular phone company or from an outside company. Your voice mail message should direct your caller to leave a message or call you at another number. Another option is to forward calls from the portable phone to another number.

Because I use a portable phone for *my* convenience, and don't give the number to anyone except my husband and my assistant, I have no need for voice mail.

### Keeping track of your messages

Taking down and sorting messages from a phone while you're working in the car, much less driving in it, is an exercise in self-discipline! It's extremely easy to misplace information and fail to follow up on important items. Whenever possible, listen to messages while you're sitting still, so that you can record the messages while you listen. There is more than one way to do this:

- Write directly into your calendar.

- Have a separate loose-leaf notebook for telephone messages.

- If you're good at extracting important information as you listen, and you have enough space in your calendar/planner, writing the message there will likely prevent you from overlooking it. Because I often write down more than I need, I make notes on a notepad, and then extract the important information from my notes into my calendar.

## Tips for Improving Your Productivity in an Office on Wheels

- Use your calendar or planner to record telephone messages, expenses, and mileage (if applicable), as well as your appointments.
- Keep all receipts together in one place, instead of having some at home and some at the office. A designated pocket in your briefcase or purse would work.
- Use notebooks to neatly hold sales sheets, order forms or other paperwork. They're easy to transport and look professional. Alternatives: Rubbermaid sells a plastic storage clipboard (14½" x 10" x 3") which holds papers, pens and pencils, etc., as well as an Autodesk, which turns the passenger seat into a desk to hold files, equipment, supplies, and so on.
- To minimize duplication of files between your home and mobile offices, use a portable file box, available from most office supply stores, to hold papers you need to use in both places.
- You can create "action" and "reference" files in your portable system, so that you can integrate them as appropriate into your system at the office. You may find it helpful to use color to separate "reference" files from "action" files.

## Coping With Computers

If computing is essential when you're on the road, a portable computer (laptop, subnotebook or palmtop) is the answer. Be sure to take along a backup battery, as most batteries won't last long enough for a transcontinental flight—or a delay in the airport. Don't forget to bring an adapter to recharge the batteries. Some printers are compact enough to take with you, but if you rarely print, the extra weight isn't justified. In most cases you'll have access to a printer at your client's office, the business center in your hotel, or a nearby copy shop (many of which are open 24 hours). Another solution is to purchase a laptop computer with a built-in ink-jet printer. Although I've seen good-quality output from such printers, you'll have to be the judge for your purposes. (See also the list of computer accessories on page 116 to carry with you when traveling for business.)

If you need to make copies and don't want to make a trip to the copy center, consider the newest portable copier. It's the size of an egg carton, costs less than $350 with a per copy cost of under 10 cents.

If you must receive a fax, but aren't sure where you'll be at a given time, sign up for a service such as SkyFax. A

- Be sure to include a "To File" file, just as you use the "To File" box in your office, so you can identify papers that need to be incorporated into your filing system when you return to the office. Enclose a copy of your File Index for your reference.
- Make it a habit at the end of each day to determine which files you need to return to your office.
- Use plastic "milk" crates, available from home or office supply stores, to organize literature and samples and keep them from sliding all over the car. You can keep them in the trunk or line them up along the backseat, as needed.
- Create an office supply caddy to hold supplies such as a stapler, scissors, paper clips, pens, packing tape and stamps. Organizing stores and catalogs have a variety of sizes and shapes—many of them with lids.
- Keep stationery in the portable file box to keep it clean and from getting dog-eared.
- Use a note pad fastened to windshield with suction cups for jotting down quick notes.

paging system notifies you when a fax is waiting, and you can direct the document to the nearest fax or laptop with a fax modem.

## Recording Your Thoughts— Wherever You Are

I rely on a small portable tape recorder. I use it to dictate ideas that come to me as I'm driving, to summarize information I get from audiotapes I listen to while driving, and to provide instructions to my assistant about what to do with the information I've recorded. When my trip is over, I give my assistant the tape to transcribe and take action as indicated.

## Dealing With Files

I carry lots of individual files with me when I travel— one for each client and one for each city I'm visiting, and one for each project I plan to work on while on the road. I have a briefcase that opens across the top so I don't have to put it down on a flat surface in order to retrieve the files.

### Office Supplies to Take When You're on the Road

- Extra business cards
- Stationery for writing quick notes
- Pens, pencils
- Adhesive notes
- Mini-stapler
- Manila folders
- Permanent marker for addressing packages
- Pre-addressed labels (or rubber stamp) to mail packages home
- Large mailing envelopes
- Postage stamps
- Blank airbills (for overnight shipping)
- Small calculator to figure expense report (unless you use one on your computer)

**If you carry a computer:**
- Modem, connector cable and AC adapter
- RJ-11 phone cord
- Spare batteries
- Blank floppy disks

**If you're traveling overseas:**
- Passport and necessary visas
- Travelers checks, local currency
- Electrical and phone adapters

Red Dot, Inc., Portland, Oregon, 800–520–0010 sells a portable filing system—a "cross between a file cabinet and a briefcase"—that I find very useful. Ten see-through polypropylene files snap into a webbing system which folds into a custom briefcase. The sides of the briefcase zip over to allow for easy retrieval. You can remove the system from the briefcase to hang in your hotel room or on your office wall. You can also remove the pouches from the nylon straps to rearrange them or use them individually.

This system (called the Red Dot System), is also useful for people who want to get current files off the desktop, but still in sight, or for people who have small work areas and could benefit from hanging files on the wall.

The system without a case is $70; system with cases range from $99-$120.

## In The Car

For many people, particularly those in sales, the car *is* their office much of the time and they need to outfit it accordingly. It's a unique organizing challenge.

A sales representative for a carpet company called me for assistance because he frequently arrived at an appointment to discover he had left an important sample or piece of information at home. To solve the problem, he made a list of everything he ever used during the course of one week. From his list, we created a checklist he used whenever he left his office to make sure he had everything he might need with him in the car. We used large laundry baskets with clearly visible labels to organize the carpet samples by price range. Finally, a portable filebox held all the printed material he needed, and a small plastic caddy held office supplies he frequently needed.

### An in-car fax

Some business people even have fax machines in their cars. If you're wondering how that's possible: The fax machine ($800-$1,000) attaches to your cellular or portable telephone with a RJ-11 jack ($100-$150)—though some models use an "acoustic coupler," which is a Velcro

**Cautionary Note:**
*In a moving car, make sure the driving comes first!*

strap that attaches to the telephone receiver to transmit the digitized sounds. The machine runs on battery power, or can be plugged into your cigarette lighter.

If you choose to keep a fax machine in your car, you have the same choices as usual about acting on any incoming faxes: Toss, Act, or File.

### And, for security's sake

For security purposes, keep as much equipment as possible out of sight in your car's trunk. Equipment that is attached to your car is covered by your car insurance policy, while equipment that is not attached—such as portable phones and fax machines—is covered by your homeowner's policy. Check your policies' limits and deductibles to make sure that your equipment is properly insured and that you purchase the appropriate rider if necessary.

One cautionary note is appropriate: In a moving car, make sure the driving comes first!

## At the Airport

If you've got a portable phone and a portable computer, setting up a mini-office in an airport while waiting for a flight is relatively simple. You can use your portable phone in the airport just like anywhere else; for a long-distance call, just dial the number with the area code and it will be charged to your cellular phone bill. If you want to minimize telephone expenses, look for a spot near a pay phone so you can use your long distance calling card

*CATHY © Cathy Guisewite. Reprinted with permission of Universal Press Syndicate. All Rights Reserved.*

instead of your portable phone. If you expect to be in the airport for some time, look for an inactive gate for more privacy and quiet in which to think, discuss business or use the phone.

Many frequent travelers join airline "clubs" to take advantage of the lounges provided by airlines. If you don't have luggage to check, you can get your boarding pass there, and make reservation changes. The lounges provide a place to store carry-on luggage, get refreshments, make telephone calls, send faxes, and use your portable computer.

Make sure you respect your travel companions when using equipment. Make conversations as brief as possible, and remember that they are not private. There's nothing worse than being forced to listen to someone else loudly carry on their business when you're trying to get something done or take a well-deserved nap.

If you're concerned about the privacy of your computer screen, you can purchase a privacy/antiglare filter which allows you to view the screen only if you are sitting directly in front of it.

## *Greetings From the Airport*

• • • • • • • • • • • • • • • • • • • • • • • • •

One of my favorite airport activities while waiting for airplanes is shopping for greeting cards. There's always a newsstand near the gate where I can use that 15 minutes before I get on the plane—and it's less fattening than eating an ice cream cone! Often I write personal notes on the plane and mail them at my next stop. If the cards are for a particular event in the future, or if I just want to have one on hand, I put them in the "To File" folder that I carry with me when I travel and file them with my other cards when I return to my office.

## *On the Airplane*

Airline regulations require that you not use portable electronic equipment during take-off and landing. Cellular telephones are not allowed at any time, because of the possibility of interfering with airplane communication systems.

Many airplanes have telephones in the seats which you can access with your credit card. GTE's AirFone and AT&T's AirOne can be used to transfer data while in the air. Don't try to send large files, and don't expect to connect at anything beyond 2,400 bps (baud per second). For data transmission, phone companies charge for a set-up and per minute use.

## *In Your Hotel Room*

Hotels are (finally!) becoming more business-traveler friendly.

When making your hotel reservations check out what facilities and equipment are available, both in the room and nearby.

Most hotels have business centers in the hotel which can provide virtually any business service you might need—but usually at a hefty price. Nonetheless, because time is often a precious commodity when you are traveling, it may be well worth the cost. Hotel concierges can also be helpful in locating services you might need.

### After you check in

Start by setting up a mini-office in your hotel room. Put the wastebasket next to your "desk" so you can throw out excess paper as often as possible. Since paper will pile up—probably in an ever-heavier briefcase or other carry-on bag—try to take action at the end of each day. If you are expecting telephone calls, check out the phone situation. Does your hotel room phone have call waiting? Does it have voice mail? If so, how do you access your messages? Make sure you have a message pad and a pencil by the phone.

For more on staying organized and handling all the various kinds of the paperwork you accumulate while traveling for business, see the next section, **"When You Attend a Convention."** There's probably no better example of potential paperwork chaos and overburden than when you attend a convention. The strategies outlined in that discussion will serve you well on any business trip.

# Attending a Convention

You know how it happens: You walk around the exhibit hall and pick up samples, brochures, business cards, order forms. You attend seminars and make notes, get handouts—and (yikes!) more business cards. You return to your hotel room and retrieve voice-mail messages from your room phone *and* your office phone, e-mail messages on your portable computer and faxes under your door. Then, of course, there are the receipts.

You return home with every intention of organizing all the material, but you're greeted by a stack of paper that accumulated while you were away—and it looks more threatening than the bags you brought home from the convention. So you stack the stuff from the convention on a shelf in your office, planning to get to them later. After several weeks, you're tired of looking at the stack, so you put the papers in a file labeled something like "Association Meeting—Chicago—1996" which is probably in front of one labeled "Association Meeting—Los Angeles—1995!" Of course, you never look at the material again.

## Make a Plan Before You Go

Read the material provided by the meeting planner, and decide which seminars and events you want to attend. If you can't attend a session but want the information, you may be able to get an audiotape.

Make a list of your objectives and rank them in order of importance. Use your calendar to schedule your time—write in pencil so you can make changes as necessary. One convention attendee told me she organized her purchase orders in the order she planned to visit booths to help keep to her schedule.

If other people from your organization will be going, use the "divide and conquer" technique. Plan your schedules together to get the most for your time and money.

If making contact with specific people is a priority, begin making plans *before* you go. For example, call and invite the person to have breakfast with you.

If you're combining business and pleasure on this trip and bringing along family members, make sure they know what to expect in terms of what to wear, when they can expect to attend functions with you, and when they'll be on their own. Make child-care arrangements before you arrive.

Be prepared to create an office in your hotel room. Pack some office supplies, and be sure to take a notebook, or use a section of your calendar, so all the notes you write while you're there will be in one place.

Attending a convention can be exhausting. By all means make sure you'll be as physically comfortable as possible. Convention and hotel rooms are often cold—be prepared. This is *not* a good time to break in new shoes. If you expect to pick up lots of catalogs or other heavy items, a backpack may come in very handy. A fanny pack is great for business cards, your hotel room key, a credit card, or other small items.

## During the Convention

Once you get to the convention, you're ready to take advantage of your advance planning. Keep the materials you collect organized as you go, and the convention—and the days afterward—will be much more pleasant.

### Keeping the paper organized

Start by setting up a mini-office in your hotel. As you attend the meetings, carry one file folder labeled "Act" and another labeled "File." Remember that every piece of paper you collect will require one of three actions: Toss, Act, or File. Every time you go by a wastebasket, check to see if you're carrying something with you that should be there!

Many of the pieces of paper you collect at the convention do not require immediate action, but contain information that might be useful in the future. These go in your "To File" file. Ask yourself the (by now familiar) question: "If I want this information again, what word will I think of first?" Write the answer to the question in the upper right hand corner. If you already have a File Index, take it with you to the convention, so you won't create a file for "Resumés" when you already have "Bios." If you don't have a File Index, this is an excellent opportunity to start one.

The remaining pieces of paper require your action. Ask yourself, "What is the next action I want to take on this piece of paper?" Write the answer in the upper right hand corner, and then when you have some time at a break or back in your hotel room, decide how you'll handle that action. If you have someone to whom you can delegate action, create a file for that person, and put the paper there. If you need to take the action by a certain day, put a reminder in your calendar.

### Catalogs

As you review catalogs you've collected, note on the front cover any items of interest so you don't have go back through them again.

### Shipping things home

Use preprinted address labels to ship back items that are too heavy to carry home in your luggage. If you're going to be away for several days, and you have an assistant back at the office, ship by overnight service any papers that can be handled while you're away.

### Organizing business cards

- Make sure you use one pocket for your cards and another for other people's cards.

- Note on all business cards the date and place you got them.

- Don't hesitate to throw away cards from people you know you won't ever contact.

- If no action is required and you, or someone else, is going to enter the cards in a card file or computer program, identify the key retrieval word by asking yourself, "If I wanted to contact this person again, what word would I think of first?" Put them all together in one place—a briefcase pocket, or an envelope in a "Computer Entry" action file.

- If you want to take an action, put it in the appropriate "action" file. For example, if you want to call for an appointment, make a note in your calendar on the day you plan to make the call, and file the business card in "Call"—or toss in the wastebasket if you recorded all the information you need elsewhere.

- If you want to send a catalog, and don't have one with you, make a note on the business card and put in the appropriate "action" file.

- If you ever use your card to write notes to yourself, make sure to put an "x" on the front of the card, so you don't accidentally give the card away.

- Consider having lightweight 3" x 5" card stock preprinted with your business-card information, leaving plenty of space in which you or its recipients can make notes.

### Expense receipts and reports

Put all expense receipts in one place, such as an envelope in your briefcase. I put the receipts in my wallet when I pay the bill or make the purchase, and at the end of the day, transfer them all to my receipt envelope. Include copies of your expense reimbursement forms. It's easier to record the purpose of an expense when you incur it than it is to reconstruct it later.

### Thank you notes

Write quick thank you notes as you go. A less than perfect "thank you" is better than no "thank you" at all!

Keep a list of the ones you have written in your calendar so you won't forget someone important or write duplicates.

### Staying focused

Refer to your "list of objectives" frequently to be sure you're on target. But don't hesitate to make changes if the situation warrants it.

## When You Get Home

**W**hen you're in the midst of something it's easy to say, "Next time I will_____." But unless you make a note of it, a year from now, when your convention rolls around again, the idea will be long forgotten. If you plan to attend this convention again next year, or even another similar kind of convention, write an "After Convention Report" to use as a guide for next year: What worked well for you, what you would do different, and why.

If you follow these suggestions, you'll return to your office having to face only one pile of the paper—the one that accumulated there while you were gone. But more importantly, those papers you collected on your trip will be a real resource, and not just another pile of postponed decisions.

# No Office
## or Sharing
## An Office

In companies where there are many telecommuters, office spaces are available to whomever needs one on a given day, referred to as "hoteling." Other professionals may find themselves working at a client site occasionally or for temporary periods of time. You'll probably be given access to a desk, chair, telephone and perhaps a computer. But you must otherwise come prepared to set up shop quickly and close it up and take it away quickly. These situations pose challenges similar to working from your car or traveling for business, and you'll find plenty of helpful tips in those sections of Chapters 12 and 13.

One other tip: When you arrive at the worksite, check in with the receptionist or whomever can help ensure that anyone who needs to find you during the day can do so. You don't want to miss telephone calls or meetings because your name isn't recognized or you're hidden away in a cubicle and no one knows where you are.

## When You Share An Office

Sharing an office has become more and more of a reality in many organizations, and in my opinion, an unfortunate one. Because of different work styles, sharing space poses one of the biggest, touchiest and extremely important organizing challenges. In order to minimize sharing, the preferable solution to overcrowding in the office would often be to create more smaller space.

If you share an office, and even more difficult, a desk, with someone on a regular basis, communication and common courtesy will be the keys to success, particularly if information and action also needs to be shared.

Here are just some of the issues that you and your officemate may need to discuss.

- **Will we share office supplies?** While you may be willing to share *some* supplies, there may be some that you won't want to share. Though space is at a premium, you'll want to find a place where you can keep those items that your officemate will honor as off-limits. For shared supplies, set up a supply checklist, and make the person who uses the last one of something responsible for replenishing the supply. (See the discussion of organizing storage closets, on page 20.)

- **If we're sharing space, but using it at different hours, how should we set it up?** Identify specific drawers for each user if at all possible.

- **Are we each going to clean off the desk at the end of our shift?** Cleaning up your stuff is highly desirable, if not absolutely necessary, in these circumstances.

- **Are we alternating use of the same chair?** If you can't each get your own desk chair, at least try to get one that allows you to change the chair height and other settings easily so you're not each fighting with it at the beginning of your shift.

- **How do we handle "work in progress" so that the person**

## When the "Highly Organized" and the "Very Casual" Work Together

• • • • • • • • • • • • • • • • • • • • • • • • •

This is probably one of the toughest assignments of all time. The key to success is

- **Sensitivity**—recognizing that one is not "right" and the other "wrong"—an overzealous neatnik can be just as irritating as a perennial slob!

- **Boundaries**—the "very casual" half of the duo needs to confine their "creativity" to specific areas.

- **Acknowledgment**—of the other persons strengths and our own weaknesses.

TAMING THE OFFICE TIGER

coming in knows where the person going out left off?
You will need a separate container—a tray, hanging file,
hot file, or drawer to contain "in progress" materials—
with notes attached to indicate status. In some instances,
it may be valuable to create a "status report" at the end of
each shift.

- **How will we handle messages for each other?** Agree on
the best way to give messages to each other. In my office,
we have a spiral-bound book for all incoming messages.
In this way, the other person can see what has come in,
and what has been completed.

## When You Move From a Traditional Office to a Work Station

**G**iven a choice, most people would prefer to have a
traditional office rather than a workstation, a.k.a. cubicle or
modular office. But many organizations are trying to put
more people in less space, and workstations are the result.
Given the fact that clutter expands to the space available
for its retention, workstations can have a positive effect by
forcing people to purge unnecessary information. At the
same time, for the individual who needs to keep a whole
library of books or other materials on hand, a workstation
can be a real challenge.

Although workstations are frequently designed to be
"one size fits all," a cost-effective option for the employer,
most can be designed to take into account individuals' various needs and workstyles, and the options are increasing
every day as the market demand increases. One woman
who moved into a new workstation discovered that the
computer dominated the corner desk area, the only part
of the workstation that could function like a traditional
desk, since it was centrally located with a kneehole area
and recessed lighting. Recognizing that she spent as much
time working on the telephone as on the computer, and
wanting space to spread her work out and read the news-
papers that her job required her to read, she moved the
computer to one side and set up her desk in the corner.

The moral here is: Don't assume that you can't adapt a workstation to your needs.

The truth is that when we have plenty of space we don't always organize the things we use in the most efficient way. A client of mine moved into her new workspace. She took things from boxes and put them on and in her desk as she used them, and much to her amazement, discovered after a month that she never used most of what she carted from her last office.

Probably the most difficult adjustment from a private office to a shared or more open workspace is the issue of privacy—or lack thereof—in telephone conversations. Learning to speak more quietly on the telephone will require vigilance and sensitivity.

Many of the space and storage issues that arise when a workplace converts to work stations are addressed in Part Four, Reorganizing the Organization.

Just prior to moving into workstations might be a great time to:

- Establish a company-wide File Clean-Out Day

- Set up a department-wide supply closet.

- Plan a department-wide library to which everyone can contribute books and other materials (presuming you can also assign someone to keep that library organized).

- Assess the need for off-site storage of archival materials or reference files.

# Reorganizing the Organization

# Assessing
# Your System

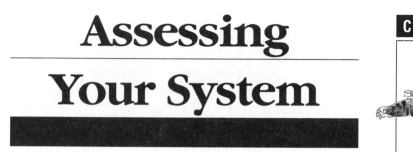
**A**n association once hired me to work with an employee about to be fired. At the last minute, the association president had second thoughts and called me to evaluate whether that was a fair action. I discovered one demoralized and poorly-trained employee, three bright, but very disorganized managers, and a disastrous filing system that didn't serve any of them.

I provided organizing skills training for each of the individuals, and we designed and implemented an effective filing system for the department. The result was a productive assistant who enjoys her job, three managers who feel they have adequate staff support and information when they need it—and file drawers that are 50% empty!

In 17 years as a consultant to individuals and businesses I've discovered that in many cases individuals are disorganized because their department or company is disorganized. Early in my career I often worked with individuals trying to make the best of a bad situation. Now I know that if the *organization* is not organized, it is virtually impossible for an *individual* to be successfully organized in the long run. That's why, if you're running a business or are charged with improving the efficiency, cost-effectiveness, and productivity of all or part of your organization, you'll want to pay special attention to this section of *Taming the Office Tiger.*

## The Problem For Organizations

**W**ith the advent of computers, the business world held high hopes for the "paperless office," a catch phrase that to many implied a clutter-free and organized workplace. While Bill Gates may not allow paper into any of *his* meetings, the rest of the world is still drowning in the stuff. Although the computer can indeed eliminate paper, it has also brought paper use to unprecedented levels.

Annual sales of file cabinets leaped 29% between 1991 and 1994, according to the Business and Institutional Furniture Manufacturers' Association in Grand Rapids, Mich. Uncoated cut-sheet paper will increase 6% by the year 2000, according to BIS Strategic Decisions, a market research and consulting firm in Norwell, Mass., that focuses on information technology. If you consider 1994's base of 4.2 million tons, that number is significant.

According to the American Forest and Paper Association, U.S. paper shipments were up 40% in the past 30 years when the futurists' predictions of a paperless office were still taken seriously. "The move to a paperless office is not even discussed at our annual meetings," says Barry Polsky, spokesman for the Association. "It's not even on the agenda."

Office automation has been an issue in many organizations during the past decade. Aetna, for example, converted 435 underwriting manuals in its property and casualty division into electronic files, eliminating 87 million pages of paper. But there's a flip side: Aetna still processes 100 million health claims a year, 80% of which come in on paper. Company reports—generated, ironically, by computer—were responsible for 1 billion printed pages in 1994.

So if we have the technical capability for a paperless office, why are we still swamped with paper?

*DILBERT reprinted by permission of United Features Syndicate, Inc.*

Ironically, because of the capability of computers, we can generate documents like never before. We can do things like:

- **Create "new and improved" reports that, all too often, few people need, want, understand or use.** Before creating a report it's important to identify whether it'll give you information you really need to know.

- **Fine-tune documents endlessly and with ease**, so we end up with multiple drafts *and* a final copy.

- **Create our own marketing materials**. In the past, sending a newsletter to clients was often financially and logistically impossible. But with the advent of desktop publishing, it's a reality, and because of competition, it's often a necessity. As a result, I have even more information to organize.

Another contributing factor to the paper pile-up is people's unwillingness to rely on computers. Many of us still like pen and paper for note-taking. Paper is more portable, and not everyone is able or willing to carry a portable computer. Even as products such as Lotus Notes make collaborative computing a reality, the savviest of executives continue to print out their documents.

Carolyn Ticknor, vice-president and general manager of HP's LaserJet Solutions Group, says their research with children who have grown up with personal computers shows that, for them, information isn't personal until it's put on paper. "When they read something on a screen off the Internet, it's like a broadcast to everyone. When they dropped it down on paper it became theirs."

But perhaps the most significant factor in organizing the office is that now, in addition to organizing paper, we have to organize our technology. Which of us hasn't sat in front of a computer screen scrolling up and down, going from window to window, searching for a document that's in there *somewhere!* Or agonized over whether to keep that vital information on computer, or on hard copy, or both?

The result? Uncontrolled information that's a burden, not a resource.

From a survey of 200 executives of large companies commissioned by Accountemps Inc., executives waste 10.7% of their total work time because they or their assistants can't find something. Assuming a 40-hour work week, that's the equivalent of 5 ½ work weeks a year.

Dan Stamp, president of Priority Management Systems, a consulting/training firm in Bellevue, Wash., says the average office worker has 36 hours of work stacked on his or her desk on an average day—and only 90 minutes to spend on it. Yet the average executive wastes 45 minutes a day searching for something lost on a desk.

An October, 1994 article in North Carolina's *Brunswick Beacon* stated that:

- 45 new sheets of paper are generated each day for each office worker.

- An average of 19 copies are made of each original.

- Almost 2 trillion pieces of paper are generated yearly in American offices.

- Executives spend up to six weeks each year searching for misfiled, misplaced or mislabeled paperwork.

- It costs about $120 in labor to track down a misplaced document or $250 in labor to recreate it.

- Recordkeeping constitutes more than 90 percent of all office activity.

Certainly few people today would be willing to go back to doing manually what we do electronically, but we're faced with new decisions about taming the office tiger.

## How Management Contributes to the Problem

One of the challenges of "organization" is that top management doesn't want to be bothered with it. In fact, the time it takes to say "file it" may be all the time senior management devotes to records management. This is a serious problem.

If you're a member of top management and you're reading this, then you *know* you've got a problem and you're probably getting ready to do something about it. If you're *not* a member of top management, then you may want to bring the problem to management's attention. I once worked with a law firm whose files were seriously overcrowded. An obvious solution was to convert traditional drawer filing to movable open-shelf filing, which holds more records in less space. In the process of transferring the files from drawers to the new units, I discovered huge files with excessive duplication. Many files could have been reduced 75% just by purging and eliminating the duplicates. Some files were more than 25 years old.

When I told my client, he said his time was too valuable to spend purging files. When I suggested he hire a law student, who could exercise some informed judgment about what to throw out, he responded, "Nobody can remove anything from the files except me." He felt he was too important to do the job himself, but no one else was important enough. So his files grew—and so did his original problem.

> ## If They Had Only Written It Down
>
> • • • • • • • • • • • • • • • • • • • • • • • • •
>
> The receptionist in a hair salon left after 17 years. Although she was the lowest-paid employee in the company, it took only days to discover that the information she had accumulated about the day-to-day workings of the business was invaluable. She was the one who knew which vendor was the most reliable, which catalog had that special product that a long-time client ordered every six months, and who to call if the soda machine wouldn't give back change. Unfortunately, she had gathered the information in her head and took it with her when she left.

## The Solution

As we discussed earlier in this book, organizing in and of itself has no intrinsic value. Highly organized businesses have gone bankrupt. Highly organized employees have lost their jobs. Organization is not the key to success—knowing what is important is. But organizing will help a company accomplish what is important to the company's principals, and do so with less money, time, and effort. It's a form of the old chicken-and-egg question. I've worked with organizations that weren't clear about what information was important, but organizing their information (beginning with eliminating what they know is *not* important), helped them accomplish that.

The techniques I'm going to describe aren't complicated, but they do take time. As a result, they're often neglected until the tiger strikes, and the results can be costly. Small businesses and major corporations face "the office tiger." Some days it sleeps, some days it merely stalks around, and then—when the auditors appear or a key person falls ill—it pounces.

This part of the book is about what steps you—as a self-employed person, business owner, executive, department manager, or supervisor—can take now to minimize the danger in your organization later. The result will be more than an insurance policy, for you will increase productivity and profit immediately.

---

## Sample Records Inventory Worksheets

• • • • • • • • • • • • • • • • • • • • • • • •

To make sure you get consistent information from your records inventory, design a form that includes such information as:

- Name of organization.

- Name of department or division, if appropriate.

- Location of file (for example, "fifth-floor supply room").

- Type of file (for example, cabinet—vertical or lateral, desk drawer, book shelf).

- Filing method used (alphabetic, numeric, other).

- Name of file category—i.e., "Accounting" or "Personnel."

- Contents of file category in generic terms, if that's not clear from the title.

- Specific file names (according to the file labels on top of the manila folders).

---

## *Identify Your Information Resources*

I can ask any manager, "What are your human resources?" and I'll get an organization chart. I can ask, "What are your financial resources?" and I'll get a budget. But if I ask, "What are your information resources?" I get a blank stare.

Stop and think about it. *Every* business, from a widget manufacturer to a doctor's office, depends on shared information. Human resources come and go, and financial resources change. But everyone has, wants or needs information, and that information *must* continue to flow in an organized way, despite changes in the workplace, or the business will suffer and eventually fail. An unexpected absence due to restructuring, accident or illness makes it essential for management and support staff to work together to develop a system that both can use and understand.

In most businesses, few decisions are made about how to structure the system, or how to allow for, or control, growth. Before long, what was intended to be a resource becomes a burden. One person thinks the information should be filed under "Cars," another thinks it's "Automobiles," and still another thinks it's "Vehicles." It becomes difficult to find *anything*. Before long, information that's important stays on the desks and in the offices of individual employees. The central filing system becomes a dumping ground for paper that probably could have gone in the wastebasket! Now, anyone who wants to find something must roam from office to office or send out a desperate e-mail message asking, "Has anyone seen..?"

A similar situation has evolved with computers. At the onset of the computer age we had a mainframe filing system that demanded that people enter data in a uniform way, just as we used to have "Mabel" in Central Files to organize the paper filing system. Many companies teeter on the edge of an information management disaster because hundreds of personal computers have been organized by individuals who weren't taught to organize their computer any better than they were taught how to organize their filing system.

## Missed Opportunities

The manager of a mortgage company wanted to hire a new loan officer, but he couldn't persuade the individual he wanted to join the company. Several months later, talking with the prospective employee, he was shocked to discover why. "I decided not to join your company because of the way the office looked," he said. "I felt the office looked out of control, and I was afraid to join the fray." The manager decided that if his office looked that way to a potential employee, it must also look that way to a potential customer— and he hired a professional organizer!

So, what's the state of *your* organization's information resources? Have you identified clearly to all employees what information you need to do business? What resources does it include—in your filing cabinets, computers, bookshelves, and in or on people's desks? How is it organized? How accessible is it to everyone who needs it? How fail-safe is your system for managing these resources? What happens if an employee leaves—or you have a major disaster such as a fire or an earthquake?

Use the accompanying list of questions to help you take stock of your organization's information resources.

If you're not pleased with what you discover when you answer the questions in the box below, keep reading.

## Preparing for Success

**M**ost people aren't thrilled when they hear, "We're going to organize the office." And with good reason! Frequently, one or more individuals have made attempts to reorganize the filing system, straighten the library or clean up the supply room, often resulting in confusion and failure. Although records-management programs often meet with initial resistance, it may be minimized if employees are reassured that their records won't be lost or

### Surveying Your Information Resources Management

Use the following list of questions to survey the state of information resources in your organization.

- Is there a person responsible for the information resource management in your organization or department?

- Are you comfortable that your department or organization retains the information that is legally required?

- Have you identified information that should be retained in an archive as a permanent record?

- Have you coordinated your paper-filing system with your computer-filing system—i.e. determined when it's appropriate to store something in paper or electronic form or, in some cases, both?

- Are you confident that staff members spend an appropriate amount of time filing and retrieving information?

- Are you (and others in your department or organization) confident that you could find a piece of paper or a computer document again once it's given to someone else to file?

made inaccessible in the process. In addition, you should:

**Lead by example** and organize your own area before making any announcements.

**Point out the value and purpose of such a program.** Your arguments might include:

- Getting rid of clutter.

- Spending less time looking for misfiled information.

- Simplifying the process of deciding what to keep and for how long.

- Eliminating having to explain what happened to documents in case of a lawsuit.

**Communicate effectively the goals you hope to accomplish.** They might include:

- Eliminating duplication of resources wherever possible.

- Making information easily accessible to everyone who needs it.

- Identifying vital records and ensuring their safety in case of a disaster.

- Establishing easy-to-use guidelines for how long everything should be kept.

- Is there plenty of room to file new information in the organization's filing cabinets and computer system?

- Do all cabinets have labels on the outside identifying the contents ?

- Are all computer disks labeled? Are they easy to read and well-filed so that anyone can find them when they need them?

- Do you schedule time regularly for you and your staff to purge unnecessary information from your file cabinets and computers?

- Are filing cabinets, shelves, and storage rooms free of unidentified piles of paper and disks?

- Does your organization train all new employees about the filing system?

- Can a temporary employee find information in the files when necessary?

- Would you be comfortable if your most important client saw how your filing system works?

- Is your crucial information backed up in such a way that it could be recovered in the case of an internal or external disaster?

- Increasing space by storing inactive but important records out of the way.

- Coordinating the information kept in hard copy versus in the computer system.

## Assigning The Responsibility

I've always found it interesting that companies have specialists on staff who are responsible for the computer system. (Although I've also noted that, in many cases, the system manager does little about training people about computer file management and organization.) Why shouldn't there be a similar position for non-electronic information? In very large companies, it might be a full-time position, referred to as "Information Resource Manager" or "Filing System Manager," if there's a separate person responsible for computer management. In smaller companies it could be part of someone's job or a part-time position.

The position would include the following responsibilities:

- Identifying, implementing and maintaining records retention policies.

- Analyzing existing filing systems and reorganizing them when appropriate.

- Coordinating storage of hard copy and computer files.

- Organizing an annual File Clean-Out Day.

- Training new employees about the information resources in the company.

Choose this person carefully. Find the most organized person in your office, as well as someone who:

- Has good rapport with all kinds of people.

- Is willing to look for answers if they need to.

- Is good with details.

- Can handle criticism.

- Has the ability and willingness to design and execute a plan.

You may find it necessary to hire an outside consultant to organize the office initially, and that person can train a staff member to maintain the system.

Make certain that you state your objectives clearly to your designee, that he or she understands them, and that you have a method to measure success.

## Why Paper Is the Starting Point

Perhaps our excitement about the possibilities of technology caused many companies to ignore or neglect paper records management. Yet surveys show much of our important information is still maintained on paper. Therefore the paper-filing system is the best place to begin organizing a company's information. Besides, much of the information there can probably be thrown away or put in archives, a move that is psychologically encouraging and motivates people to organize their own files.

As you begin, keep in mind that this isn't a short sprint—it's a long-distance run. Years of accumulation and postponed decisions won't disappear quickly. No one who has designed or improved a filing system would argue that it's a fast or easy task. But businesses today cannot afford to ignore that their continued success—or even survival—will be based on *team* effectiveness. And effective organization increases team effectiveness. Valuable time is wasted when employees duplicate each other's work; produce, copy, or circulate reports or messages that aren't important to everyone who receives them; or spend time looking for information that's buried on someone's desk or in their computer.

A filing system is like the foundation of a building. People may not see it, and it's not as exciting as the outside of the building or the interior decorating, but if you ignore it, eventually the rest of the building will suffer and fall. Sometimes a filing system is an indicator of the company's overall health: It often reflects the power structure, political atmosphere, communication strengths and weaknesses, and clarity of purpose within the organization. If, for example, the files are full of information used to prove that a certain transaction occurred, it may mean that customer service is weak. Employees, instead of responding to the customer's complaint about not receiving a product, spend time documenting what went wrong and whose fault it was. Unfortunately, many companies don't recognize this, or do nothing about it, until it's too late.

---

### Hire a Professional

• • • • • • • • • • • • • • • • • • • • • • • •

To find a specialist in your area to help you organize your office, call the National Association of Professional Organizers (NAPO, 1033 La Posada, Suite 220, Austin, TX 78752; 512–206–0151; fax 512–454–3036.

---

## Conduct A Records Inventory

The first step is to conduct a records inventory to identify the existing files. This should be done on a department-by-department basis. Conduct a preliminary "walk through" and sketch all offices where records are stored. Use an office blueprint if one is available. List locations (which offices) and types of equipment (legal or letter files, computers, storage cabinets, book shelves, and so on).

Inventorying files is much easier for two people than one. One person reads the names of the files, and the other enters it in a word processor, or writes it on a pad if the computer is too far away. If one of the participants is the employee who uses the files, this preliminary exercise will probably result in some files ending up in the trash (where they should have been long ago)! By simply looking at files, you may come across ones that are antiquated and disposable. At the very least, the person doing the inventory should ask the file's regular users for recommendations of files that are no longer used.

Records inventory is a big job and may take a long time. As you circulate through the department, you will certainly encounter protests and horror stories about lawsuits won because of boxes of old company files squirreled away in a retiree's garage. You'll also hear "my files are personal." But employees must be made aware that all files pertaining to the company *belong* to the organization.

It's risky to allow employees to conduct their own inventories, without the assistance of someone who will be involved in the entire process. Aside from the fact that they'll be hard-pressed to find time to do it, the information you receive may be inconsistent or incomplete.

**SPECIAL**

**SECTION**

# Establishing Retention Guidelines

**A**fter you've completed the inventory of existing files, the next step is to establish user-friendly retention guidelines. Often, offices are glutted with paper and computer files because people using them aren't given guidelines about what to keep and what to eliminate.

---

## Simplify Paper Management

· · · · · · · · · · · · · · · · · · · · · · · ·

The best way to simplify paper management is (naturally) to not create excess paperwork in the first place. A good resource to assist you in looking at these issues is *Cutting Paperwork in the Corporate Culture* by Dianna Booher ($16.95 Facts on File; 800—342—6621).

---

Ironically, some organizations do have such guidelines, but they're not communicated to the people who really need them, or not provided in a user-friendly form. One company I worked with had a guidebook that was nearly a hundred pages long, but poorly organized, and contained information most people didn't need.

As a general rule, retention guidelines are most useful when organized by department, but it's helpful to know what other departments keep. For example, in one company I discovered three departments (on the same floor) keeping information about potential meeting sites. This is unnecessary duplication and takes far too much space. In addition to keeping it in three places, they kept the

*(continued on page 148)*

## What Should You Keep and for How Long?

Here are some guidelines:

- **Annual financial statements:** Retain indefinitely.

- **Monthly financial statements** used for internal purposes: Retain for three years.

- **Bank reconciliations, voided checks, check stubs and check register tapes**: Retain for six years.

- **Books of account,** such as the general ledger and general journal: Retain indefinitely, unless posted regularly to the general ledger. ("Ledgers" refer to the actual books or the magnetic tapes, disks, or other media upon which the ledgers and journals are stored.)

- **Subsidiary ledgers:** Retain for three years.

- **Canceled, payroll and dividend checks:** Retain for six years.

- **Corporate documents,** including certificate of incorporation, corporate charter, constitution and bylaws, deeds and easements, stock, stock transfer and stockholder records, minutes of board of directors' meeting, retirement and pension records, labor contracts, licenses, patents, trademarks and registration applications: Retain indefinitely.

- **Documents substantiating fixed-asset additions,** such as the amounts and dates of additions or improvements, detail related to retirements, depreciation policies, and salvage values assigned to assets: Retain indefinitely.

- **Income tax, revenue agents' report, protests, court briefs and appeals:** Retain indefinitely.

- **Income tax payment checks:** Retain indefinitely.

- **Personnel and payroll records,** such as payments and reports to taxing authorities, including federal income tax withholding, FICA contributions, unemployment taxes and workers' compensation insurance: Retain for four years.

- **Purchase records,** including purchase orders, payment vouchers authorizing payment to vendors and vendor invoices: Retain for six years.

- **Sales records** such as invoices, monthly statements, remittance advisories, shipping papers, bills of lading and customers' purchase orders: Retain for six years.

- **Travel and entertainment records,** including account books, diaries and expense statements: Retain for six years.

information for several years when in fact, it wouldn't be wise to make a decision about a meeting space based on old information.

## *More Information About Retention Guidelines*

● ● ● ● ● ● ● ● ● ● ● ● ● ● ● ● ● ● ● ● ● ● ● ● ●

If you still need more information about retention guidelines for your organization, check with the following organizations:

- **Association for Records Managers and Administrators** (ARMA, 4200 Somerset Drive, Suite 215, Prairie Village, KS 66208; 913–341–3808). They provide valuable information including:

  Records retention guidelines by industry for $10 each.

  *EDI and American Law: A Practical Guide* by Benjamin Write, JD. (EDI is electronic data interchange, the computer-to-computer exchange of business data.) The absence of paper documentation raises evidence, statute of frauds, tax, and other legal issues. This book is particularly helpful because it describes EDI in nontechnical terms.

  Names of local ARMA Chapters where you could get local assistance.

- *Information and Records Management* by Mary Robak, Gerald F. Brown and David Stephens. Glencoe Publishing; 800–334–7344.

- Another valuable resource is: *Recordkeeping Requirements* by Donald Skupsky ($35.00 + S&H from **Information Requirements Clearinghouse,** 5600 South Quebec Street, Suite 250-C, Englewood, CO 80111; 303–721–7500).

### *Talk With Staff Members*

People who use files regularly are the best source of information when you're developing retention guidelines. Use the records inventory form discussed previously as a starting point for discussion, and determine how long people actually use the information that is kept. In many cases, employees may not know—which is exactly the reason for going through this process.

### *Talk With Your Advisors*

To further develop your retention guidelines, collect all the information you can from your accountant and general counsel about what information is legally necessary in your company (and see the accompanying box for suggestions). In some cases, your organization may belong to an industry-related association which might be able to provide additional guidelines.

## The "Originator's Rule:" The Universal Retention Guideline

It's essential to keep some information, but unnecessary and undesirable to keep duplicate information. One way to avoid this is to be sure everyone in your office understands and implements, wherever applicable, the "Originator's Rule: Whoever originates a piece of paper is responsible for its retention!"

## Document Your Recordkeeping Plan.

Once you've collected all the available information about records retention from internal and external sources, it's time to put the information in some sort of user-friendly form for each department by adding the information to your File Index.

If your company becomes involved in litigation or an audit, you'll be in a much better position to protect yourself if you produce evidence of your records-retention program. Having a formal records retention program creates consistency and indicates an honest attempt to retain important information. For example, if you're audited and you have only some records, you look sloppy at best. At worst, you give the impression that you're trying to hide something.

It's a good idea to set up and maintain a computer database of the company's records, including the location of all records and how long they must be kept. This will give you the flexibility to sort the information into various types of lists as needed.

**Originator's Rule**

*Whoever originates a piece of paper is responsible for its retention.*

CHAPTER

16

# File

# Clean-Out Day

**A**re there items in your office you'd eliminate if you had the time to do so? Sure there are! And no doubt that's true for every person in your office.

A management-endorsed "File Clean-Out Day" sends the message that managing paper effectively is an essential part of day-to-day business, and not something to relegate to "some Saturday." Depending on the nature of your business, you may do all departments on the same day, or you may need to schedule "File Clean-Out Days" on different days.

One CEO of an 80-employee company summed up the imperative pretty well: After spending a day cleaning up his own office, the CEO called everyone together for my "Taming the Paper Tiger" seminar. He introduced it by saying, "Here is a list of the crucial things you need to keep. The rest of it you don't need. You are not going to get larger cubicles, so start tossing."

If your organization hasn't *systematically* cleaned out files for several years, dedicating one day to the task will probably not be enough, but it's a good place to start.

## Organizing the Big Day

### Select the day for your "File Clean-Out Day" carefully.

Choose a time when office demands are at their lowest. Many organizations find it practical to use the same day each year. One company holds an "Annual St. Patrick's Day Clean-Out" while another calls it "Dump

150

Day." One former client has two days per year: one in April (Fool's Day) and one in October (Ghoul's Day)!

## Announce the day well in advance, and designate specific hours for beginning and ending the day.

Make certain *everyone* understands that they are expected to participate—no one is too important, too unimportant, or too busy. It's essential that management actively participate. With some clients we've done a "pilot project" with the head of a department in order to determine whether the results would be worth the investment. In this case, that person or persons can serve as role model. In all cases, it's crucial for management to demonstrate their support of the project.

In fact, one company I know uses the paper file clean-out day as a day for routine computer maintenance as well. Once the computer system is "down," no one can bury him- or herself in the computer instead of the files!

### What's Lost Is Found

• • • • • • • • • • • • • • • • • • • • • • • •

File Clean-Out Day is also a good opportunity to locate important missing documents or other items. For example, one organization was missing some issues of its newsletter, which they wanted to keep for historical reasons. By alerting staff members to this need, the organization recovered all the missing copies during File Clean-Out Day.

## Assign one person as "File Clean-Out Day" Coordinator.

Choose someone who has good rapport with the staff, is good with details, and has read this book! Ideally, it should be the person who will be assigned as information resource manager or filing system manager.

## Work with the coordinator to develop or provide materials to support the day.

These might include any existing retention guidelines, a "What to do if..." Tipsheet, and Guidelines for an effective "File Clean-Out Day." (See samples on pages 153-154)

## Hire temporary employees to answer the telephones.

Instruct staff members to notify temps if there are specific calls they need to answer.

## Provide large trash receptacles, trash bags, marking pens and labels.

Make arrangements for extra recycling boxes. One company had fluorescent orange labels printed with "Basura" ("trash" in Spanish), because the cleaning crew did not read English. Identify a specific place where staff members can leave reusable supplies and equipment for recycling by others who might need them.

## Notify the building maintenance crew that there will be extra trash on that day.

Engage their cooperation to move heavy boxes, trash barrels, and so on, as needed. It may be helpful to offer a cash bonus for their cooperation.

## Encourage staff to wear comfortable clothes.

Set an example by doing so yourself. (Some clients order T-shirts with an appropriate theme for the occasion.)

## Encourage staff to use adhesive notes on the outside of file cabinets or on groups of files.

Ask them to use the adhesive notes to indicate what further action is required, for example, "Discuss with...," "Move to...," "Type labels," and so on. These notes will be helpful in collecting information to share during the group meeting at the end of the day, during which a decision can be made about how to move ahead with the project. This might include having another clean-out day, or continuing the process on an individual basis.

## Be creative

Bring a camera for "before" and "after" photos that can be posted on bulletin boards or printed in the company

*(continued on page 156)*

## Sample "What To Do If..." Tipsheet

This hand-out should describe the nuts and bolts procedures for the day, such as where to get supplies and who to contact if there's a problem. For example,

### IF YOU NEED...

- File folders, labels, tape, etc., get them from_____.

- File boxes and file box labels (to send materials off-site). Get them from _____.

- Physical help to move boxes, contact _____.

### WHAT IF YOU...

- Have materials to be taken to file storage room?

  Only materials which have been thoroughly inventories and clearly labeled can be taken to storage. Call _____to have them picked up.

- Have materials which need to be saved but are rarely accessed?

  These materials can be sent to off-site storage. Materials must be thoroughly inventoried and clearly labeled. Off-site storage costs will be paid by_____. Call_____to get further information.

- Find materials which belong in another area?

Place the items in a box and label clearly the contents and desired destination. (Be careful not to mix boxes that should be saved with boxes of trash!)

- Find materials that aren't listed on the Retention Guidelines, and which you feel should be kept within the organization?

Mention the item on your Problem Identification Form. Leave the items in your files until the issue is resolved. If you have questions, ask_____.

### ABOUT PHONE COVERAGE

All telephones will be answered by the reception desk. Notify them if you must take a call.

### ABOUT TRASH REMOVAL

A number of points throughout the office will be designated for depositing trash which will be picked up by the cleaning crew. You may leave trash in your own workstations provided it is marked with a trash sticker. It will help the cleaning crew if you separate paper trash from other materials, such as metals, which cannot be put in the building dumpster.

**Remember:** Don't throw away file folders still in good condition. Reuse them whenever you can or take them to the designated area in the supply room.

## Six Steps to an Effective "File Clean-Out Day"

The following is a quick reminder for individuals on making the most effective use of "File Clean-Out Day." Note: You'll find much of this advice discussed in more detail in Part One of this book. In some cases, I've cross-referenced the step to the appropriate chapter.

### Step 1 - What do I need to keep?

Before keeping any file or piece of paper ask the "Art of Wastebasketry" questions described in Chapter 4:

- Does this information require my action?

- Does this information exist elsewhere?

- Is it recent enough to be useful?

- Can I identify how I would use it?

- Are there tax or legal implications? And, most importantly,

- What's the *worst possible thing* that would happen if I didn't have this piece of paper?

And, remember the "Originator's Rule," which becomes the "rule of the day:" "Whoever originates a document is responsible for its ultimate retention. Other users are responsible for keeping it only as long as *they* need it!

### Step 2 - Where do I keep it?

If you choose to keep the paper or the file, put it in one of the following major categories: (See Chapters 3, 4, and 8)

- **Action files,** which you should store in or on your desk or in the cabinet or shelf near your desk.

- **Current reference files,** which are used or could be used for current projects.

- **Outdated reference (historical or archival) files**, which aren't necessary for current projects, but are desirable or necessary for historical or legal reasons.

### Step 3 - How do I keep it?

(See Chapter 3)

- **Use hanging files whenever possible.** If you take out only the piece of paper you need from the file, no manila file is necessary. If you take the file out of the cabinet, use a manila file inside.

- **If manila files are used for subdivisions within a hanging file,** put the main title *and* subtitle on manila files. When files become thick, use box-bottom files.

- **Use color *only* if it "tells a story,"** for example, all administrative files are red, and all program files are green.

- **Replace paper clips** with staples or the smallest possible binder clip.

- **Stamp or write "FILE COPY: DO NOT REMOVE"** when applicable. Place the original used for making additional copies (of a form, for example) in a sheet protector.

- **Be certain all papers have a date;** file them in chronological order, with the most recent item on top.

- **When using plastic tabs,** choose clear or

light colors (dark-colored ones are difficult to read). Place plastic tabs on the *front* of hanging files. Stagger the tabs across the tops of the files so all labels are visible when the drawer is open.

- **When using manila files,** place the file name as close to the top of the tab as possible. If using colored labels, put the file name on the top and the color on the bottom. This technique minimizes the possibility of filed papers obscuring the file title.

- **If this is a new file title,** be sure to add it to your File Index.

- **Leave at least 3" of space in each drawer** for expansion.

- **Label the outside of file cabinets** with the contents.

## Step 4 - What shall I call it?

Check the existing File Index to see if an appropriate file already exists for the papers you want to file. If not, establish a new file by asking "What word would I think of *first* if I wanted or needed to retrieve this information?"

If you don't have a File Index, create one now. Creating the Index as you go, instead of going back and doing it later, will take less time, and will eliminate making a file for "Auto" when you already have "Car."

## Step 5 - Evaluating your day's accomplishments

- Allow thirty minutes at the end of the day to assess your progress: How much more time do you need to finish the project? When will you do it?

- What retention questions came up and who can answer them?

- Label all piles and files so you can easily access information until you can get everything in its final location.

## Step 6 - Maintenance

Two things are essential for maintaining the accomplishments of your File "Clean-Out Day:"

1. **Make the File Index "user-friendly"** (You probably will not have time to complete this on "File Clean-Out Day," but schedule time to do it as soon as possible to get the most return on the time you spent cleaning out.)

- Single space the index, except between letters of the alphabet, to minimize the number of pages.

- Use the File Index to keep track of oversized materials, books, or other materials, noting their location.

- Keep a copy of the File Index near the file cabinet or at the desk of everyone who uses the files.

- Update the File Index regularly.

2. **Note the required retention guideline** beside each category whenever possible.

This will make file clean-out easier next time.

newsletter. Some organizations even provide T-shirts for the occasion. Consider awards for "the oldest," "the funniest," "the strangest," and so on. (Here's a true example: One office found the back half of a donkey pinata!) Let staff members keep their choice of stuff that would have been thrown out, such as notebooks or reference materials.

---

## *Comfort While Cleaning Out*

• • • • • • • • • • • • • • • • • • • • • • •

Cleaning files is physically (and mentally) tiring. To maximize your energy, be as physically comfortable as possible:

• Wear comfortable shoes.

• Sit in a chair in front of the files, or bring files to your desk.

• Use good lifting techniques to avoid back strain.

• Throw trash into your wastebasket and then empty that into a large bin or recycling box.

---

### Serve a simple quality lunch for everyone

This will encourage communication among staff about what needs to be done, and enables people to return to the task at hand as soon as possible. It also promotes camaraderie—everyone has a story to share about their experiences!

### Gather all staff together 30 minutes before the designated ending time.

Ask them to fill out evaluation forms regarding their day's experience. Ask these questions:

• What questions do you have as a result of cleaning out your files?

• How much more time do you need to finish this job?

• How could we improve this day?

Genuinely thank all employees for their contribution to this important effort.

### Finally, management should meet with the Coordinator

Discuss the evaluation forms submitted by the staff and determine what steps to take next, and when. These might include:

• Scheduling the next "File Clean-Out Day."

- Identifying who will be responsible for getting answers to questions that arose during the process.

- Shifting files from one department to another.

- Ordering new equipment.

- Updating the file retention guidelines.

Compile statistics to document the amount of materials removed from the files. Publicize your results and your success!

## Recycling

In my early years of organizing "File Clean-Out Days," before many organizations were actively involved in recycling, participants would say "Oh, look at all those trees we're wasting!" when they saw the dumpsters filling up. I responded, "Do you think we're saving them by keeping the paper in the files?" Now, when we bring in recycling containers, participants say, "Oh, look at all the trees we're saving!"

If you haven't already, File Clean-Out Day is an excellent opportunity to implement, or improve, your recycling practices. This includes not only paper, but equipment, unneeded supplies and inventory.

### Computer equipment

Computer equipment, that's too old or slow for your business might be perfect for a "computerless" nonprofit business that will benefit from the ability to perform even simple word processing. Listed below are several organizations that accept donations of old computers. After being refurbished, they are placed in schools and nonprofit organizations, as well as with individuals. You could also check with your local schools and nonprofit organizations to see whether they accept used equipment.

- The Computers for Schools Program, in La Jolla, Cal. (800–939–6000)

- The Computer Recycling Center, in Mountain View, Cal. (415–428–3700)

- The East-West Foundation, in Boston. (617–542–1234)

- The National Christina Foundation, in New York. (800–274–7846)

- The Computer Reclamation Inc., in Silver Spring, Md. (TCRI; 301–495–0280)

### Excess inventory

National Association for the Exchange of Industrial Resources, in Galesburg, Ill. (NAEIR; Galesburg, IL; 309–343–0704) is a nonprofit organization that acts as a go-between for its members and companies wishing to make tax-deductible donations of excess inventory.

## "File Clean-Out Day" for Your Computer

**C**omputer files also need to be purged—*but not on the same day as your paper files.* Not only will there not be enough time, but it's difficult to work with both mediums simultaneously. However, the process is the same as that described for hard copy files.

• Eliminate unnecessary documents whenever possible.

• If your computer file system is not organized, and you do not have time to go through all old documents, start over.

• Set up a system for organizing the new documents by creating subdirectories. These might include project names, client names, forms, organizations, topics of interest.

• When a subdirectory contains too many files to be easily manageable, create another subdirectory. For example, if a directory for a particular client becomes unmanageable, create a subdirectory for each department, or project, related to that client. (See Chapter 10 for information on computer filing.)

*DILBERT reprinted by permission of United Features Syndicate, Inc.*

# Improving (or Creating) Your New Filing System

**O**kay, now you've eliminated unnecessary information. The next step is to organize what you *do* need to keep. In many offices, the filing systems have more or less evolved without any real planning.

## Decide Who Will Design the System

As we discussed earlier, it's essential to designate one person responsible for making sure the filing system is effective. If a File Systems Manager (or Information Resources Manager or Records Resource Manager) has been designated, this person should work with each department to identify and assist in the design and implementation of the system. It can be one person, or a "task force," depending on the needs of the department or organization.

## Analyze the Current System Using Your Organization's File Index

Use the File Indexes created as a result of "File Clean-Out Day." The easiest way to analyze a system is by looking at the current file index, rather than the drawers

159

themselves, because by the time you get to the end of the second drawer, you won't remember what was in the first drawer—much less many offices full of file drawers.

Can you tell by looking at the index how to quickly file or find any document in your department? If your system is in relatively good shape, you and other staff members may only need to rearrange a few files. But, if yours is like most organizations I've seen, a major overhaul may be in order. In that case, the best approach might be to start over. Here are some suggestions:

## First design your system on paper, by creating or revising the department File Index

Human nature is such that we "buy in" to a system when we have the opportunity to participate in its design, so it'll be helpful to at least talk with employees to identify what they like and don't like about the existing system.

One of the major contributors to confusing filing systems is having too many categories. Put information in its largest general categories first. These might include: Administration, Clients, Financial, and Resources. I create a new category when that subject takes up more than one-half of a file drawer. For example, if all the information you have about travel takes only a few files, they would be filed under "T" in "Administration." I keep extensive information about travel, so I've created a "Travel" category in a separate drawer.

After you've identified the major categories, assign a number to each category. For example, "Accounting Information" could be assigned "1;" Administrative files could be assigned "2," and so on. Then go through your index of all the existing files, deleting or adding new files when appropriate, and beside each file title, mark the number (1 or 2, etc.) of the major category in which that file belongs. Now redo the Index by putting all "1s" together, all "2s" together, and alphabetize them within their categories.

Then create your new File Index by reorganizing all like file titles in the most appropriate way. Apply the following guidelines:

• Alphabetical filing systems, such as by name, place, or

subject. Use basic alphabetizing rules:

- Alphabetize last names first, e.g., "Adamson, Ann."

- Consider prefixes as part of name, e.g., "St. John, Oliver."

- Arrange hyphenated names as written, e.g., "First-Hartling, Laura."

- Arrange company names as written, e.g., "Manhattan School of Music."

- Disregard "The" at the beginning of a name, e.g., "The Center for Advanced Studies" is indexed as "Center for Advanced Studies, (The)."

- Political divisions are indexed with major name first, e.g., "U.S. Department of Agriculture" is indexed as "United States Government, Agriculture (Dept. Of)."

## Make the physical files match the system you created

Now you can make your physical files match the new File Index you created by pulling together physically all the files assigned "1," all files assigned "2" and so on.

**Separate out old records that are vital, but could be useful.** Put the *vital* records in a safe storage place, preferably off-site, and put the old records someplace other than prime office space. If you choose an off-site facility to store inactive records, make sure it's clean, climate-controlled, secure, and insulated. It should be managed by a storage company that is bonded and insured against fire and flood.

Label boxes or files clearly, indicating the contents and destruction date. Failure to select a destruction (or review) date will mean unnecessary ongoing storage expense and a *massive* cleanup project in the future. Keep a record of stored files in an easily accessible place (e.g., in your administrative files under "Records Storage-off-site") so it can be referenced and updated when necessary.

# Centralized Vs. Decentralized Files

Despite resistance to the idea of centralizing files, information kept in one place increases control over the filing system, minimizes misfiles and lost documents, and makes routine destruction less complicated.

Not so long ago, most organizations had a "central filing system" controlled by one person. If you wanted a piece of paper, you had to ask "Mabel." When you were finished, you returned the paper to "Mabel," confident that she'd find it for you if you needed it again. Then many businesses found it necessary to reduce office space and personnel. There was no longer space for a central file room, nor money for "Mabel." Soon filing cabinets were tucked in corners around the office, and people all around the company began filling them with paper. Before long, those cabinets were a dumping ground for papers no one really cared about, while individual offices filled up with paper because their occupants were afraid to use the "central" files. Sound familiar?

Historically, "central" files refer to a specific location, such as a file room or a large bank of files, where everyone files information that is of use to the department. Even if "Mabel" was still around, space constraints make it difficult to maintain a central location for files.

## The Matter of Forms

Every office has forms. In organizing an office, one of the first steps I take is to request from each employee a copy of every form they use. I get several versions of the same form, as well as forms that no one is using. Here's a simple solution:

- **Gather all forms together in a central location.** (Employees can still keep copies of frequently used forms at their desks.) If there are only a few forms, they can be filed in the administrative files under "F." If there are many forms, assign one drawer and label it "Forms." File the forms alphabetically, and create an index of forms that will be posted in the front of the drawer. On the index, note each form's official name.

- **Keep one copy of each form in a page protector.** Label "File Copy—Do Not Remove" to minimize the possibility of someone taking the last copy. When applicable, make a note of where new forms can be obtained.

- **In many cases, forms are now computerized.** It's equally important for everyone to know how those are filed in the computer. If your organization has some forms in hard copy and some in the computer, use the Forms Index to indicate both types and their location. If your organization's forms are entirely computerized, create a subdirectory called "Forms."

However, the concept is still possible by developing a master plan of the system and clearly identifying file cabinets in various locations. I often refer to it as a "*Centrally Understood* Filing System."

This simply means that the files, as well as other kinds of resources, are located *physically* in the most logical place for the people using them but are available for anyone who needs them.

## The Final Step: Your Information Resource Directory

Remember when we discussed the value of an organization chart to track human resources and a budget to track financial resources? The information found in filing systems and computers, on bookshelves and desks, is also valuable and essential to an organization and to its employees. All organizations should be able to easily identify those resources, just as they can identify their personnel and financial resources. I call this an "Information Resource Directory."

After you've organized your hard copy and computer files, look at the other sources of information in your office

### Saving on Subscriptions

One client had an entire room full of newsletters, magazines, audio and videotapes. We inventoried the contents of the room, noting the names of publications, not the specific issues on hand. We circulated the resulting list and asked employees to put a check by those they used. More than 80% of the publications on the list had no check! Consider the cost of purchasing those publications, organizing them, and then storing them. This client saved plenty just by eliminating the excess.

that need to be organized: Computer disks or tapes, microfilm, card files, books, audiotapes, videotapes, and notebooks are just a few possibilities.

For example, if several employees receive the same publications, set up a central library and eliminate the duplicate subscriptions. Or, if everyone maintains a personal file of interoffice memos, set up a central file (or binder) where they are arranged by subject, date, or author.

Group resources together by category; i.e., books, pamphlets, notebooks, audiotapes and videotapes, etc. Group them by subject, such as "Advertising" or "Management." You may choose to alphabetize them within the category, but in my experience, it's not worth the time. However, you can use a colored dot on the binding to indicate the subject. For example, all management books have red dots, while all marketing books would have a yellow dot. This will encourage people to return them to the proper location.

Apply the same organizing principles to these items as you did to the traditional files. These include:

- Eliminate unnecessary items by discarding, recycling, or returning.

- Put like items together.

- Determine the most appropriate location for those items—e.g., storage room, mail room, bookshelves in X's office, cupboard in Y's office, etc.

- Identify the best container for the items—e.g., notebook, magazine-type containers, closed boxes, open baskets, etc.

- Label notebooks, shelves, cupboards, and containers clearly.

## Finally, make a list of all resources, divide it into categories, and place in a loose-leaf notebook

These categories might include: hard copy files, computer files, book shelves, storage cabinets, and even individual desks, if the information located there might be

*CATHY, © Cathy Guisewite. Reprinted with permission of Universal Press Syndicate. All Rights Reserved.*

needed by other members of the organization.

This notebook should be easily available to all people who use the information resources in your office.

Be sure to update the Information Resource Directory at least once a year when you complete your annual file clean-out day.

Imagine how it would feel to be able to present this document to a new employee! A graduate student told me that he spent the first three weeks of an internship looking for information he needed to complete the project he was hired to do. Obviously, this was not necessary, certainly not cost effective, and could have been avoided if the organization had had an information resource directory.

## 6 Tips for Organizing the Organization

1. Assign someone to be responsible for organizing the information.

2. Identify the information that is essential to your organization and establish retention guidelines.

3. Conduct a "File Clean-Out Day," and repeat at least annually.

4. Complete an inventory of the existing files and create user-friendly file indexes.

5. Complete an inventory and create an index of other types of information.

6. Use your inventory of files and other types of information to create an Information Resource Directory which is updated at least annually.

## On the Road to Success

Remember: In every organizing process, things might get worse before they get better. This is natural and unavoidable.

It would be wonderful if we could stop the telephones, the mail, and the interruptions for a few days—or weeks—while we get organized, but in the real world that's not possible. This means that you may have to organize in stages.

As you proceed, continually ask yourself, "Does this work? Do I like it?"—and, if what you are organizing affects the people around you, "Does it work for others?" If the answer to any of those questions is "No," keep trying—and don't be afraid to ask for help if you need it.

There's no glamour in getting organized, but it's a critical component of a healthy, productive office. My experience is that the more organized an individual or an organization becomes, the more willing either one is to toss stuff out. We tend to think that piles of disorganized information contain information that would be very useful if only we could find it. It's only after we get the information organized that we can measure whether or not we will really use it.

Frequently, clients ask me, "How long is this project going to take?" The answer is often, "I don't know, but I do know that the longer you wait, the longer it will take and the more difficult it will be—so the sooner you begin, the better." I know you will reap rewards for your effort!

*If you have questions about the ideas presented in this book, or would like information about speaking or consulting services or other organizing products, please feel free to contact Hemphill & Associates, Inc., 1464 Garner Station Blvd, #330, Raleigh, NC 27603, 919-834-8510 or 76443,3014@Compuserve.com.*